Cat
Basics

Cat

The essential guide to caring for your cat

Basics

Caroline Davis

hamlyn

A Pyramid Paperback

First published in Great Britain in 2007 by
Hamlyn, a division of Octopus Publishing Group Ltd
2–4 Heron Quays, London E14 4JP

This material was previously published as *Essential Cat*.

Distributed in the United States and Canada by
Sterling Publishing Co., Inc.
387 Park Avenue South, New York, NY 10016–8810

ISBN-13: 978-0-600-61470-8
ISBN-10: 0-600-61470-0

A CIP catalogue record for this book is available from the
British Library

Printed in China

10 9 8 7 6 5 4 3 2 1

The advice given here should not be used as a substitute for
that of a veterinary surgeon. No cats or kittens were harmed
in the making of this book. In this book, unless the information provided is specifically for female cats, cats are referred
to throughout as 'he'. The information is equally applicable to
both male and female cats, unless otherwise specified.

CONTENTS

INTRODUCTION

'A home without a cat, and a well-fed, well-petted and properly revered cat, may be a perfect home, perhaps, but how can it prove its title?' questioned the American author Mark Twain (1835–1910) – and he had a point. Somehow, as any cat lover will confirm, a cat does seem to make a home feel more welcoming, more friendly and even safer and more secure.

Even those who profess not to like cats tend to change their opinion once they get to know what makes cats tick. For those who adore felines in whatever shape or form they present themselves, life is simply not complete without a cat galloping to greet them, chirruping and sinuously weaving around their legs for attention and then, later, curling up, relaxed and purring, on their laps, for a comforting mutual-admiration session.

CHOOSING A CAT

Cats differ greatly in their needs, personalities and ideal living situations, so it is important to choose a cat who will be happy to live with you, and who you will be proud to own. Do you have time for the daily grooming needed by a longhaired cat? Do you want a sociable, affectionate cat or a more independent companion? Would a more mature cat be a more appropriate addition to your household than a kitten? Be sure to make an informed choice by reading the following pages carefully.

Why have a cat?

In Britain and the USA, cats now outnumber dogs as the most popular pet. Perhaps the main reasons for this are their relative independence and ability to exercise and relieve themselves outside without human assistance. This makes them less of a tie than dogs, who need companionship and someone to take them out on a regular basis. A cat can also be as affectionate as any dog, and just as much fun to play with.

Companionship

A cat not only provides good company, he also imparts a sense of peace and tranquillity in a chaotic, stressed world. Research has shown that having a cat – or another pet – can help us relax and recover from illness, as well as keep us alert and lively as we age.

Cats are naturally self-reliant animals, although we need to protect them in urban

With today's high standards in veterinary medicine and feline food, pet cats can live well into their teens – and even longer.

areas where they are especially vulnerable to passing traffic. Cats are more independent by nature than dogs, but they can prove to be very loyal and rewarding companions, and will ask for little in return except food, shelter and affection.

Exercise

In general, cats exercise themselves through hunting (if allowed outside) and play. Some owners, whether they live in urban or rural areas, build an enclosed run in their gardens or yards so that their cat can have freedom and fresh air without risking his safety. Interactive play with your cat on a daily basis will also help strengthen the bond between you and keep him occupied (and less prone to behavioural problems).

Daily care

In comparison with some other household pets, a cat's daily needs are relatively few – longhaired breeds are an exception to this, as they need daily brushing to prevent coat and skin problems. Cats are usually fastidious about grooming and washing themselves, so bathing is not normally necessary, but a daily brushing will help keep shed hairs in the house to a minimum.

Maintenance costs

Cats are inexpensive to keep. Other than food and cat litter on a weekly basis, the only other regular expenses will be parasite treatments as recommended by a vet, annual vaccinations against the diseases cats are susceptible to, a veterinary health check every 12 months, and toys to play with (you will find small scrunched-up balls of paper and ping-pong balls will do the job admirably). Although an optional expense, pet insurance can be a wise investment – should your pet suffer an accident or illness, any necessary veterinary treatment could cost a large amount.

Advantages

Cats don't bark and howl, so your neighbours won't be upset on that score, which is especially important if you live in a highly populated, built-up area. As long as he is fed regularly, he has clean, fresh water

Cats make great playmates for people of all ages. Interactive play with your cat provides entertainment for you both and ensures he gets sufficient exercise.

available to drink, his litter tray is kept clean and he has a safe area in which to exercise and rest, plus some toys to play with, then a cat will be content. If he is sociable and has a warm lap to sit on and a gentle hand to stroke him now and again, he will be a very happy cat, keen to reciprocate his owner's affection.

Type of accommodation

Cats can live quite happily in most homes. Many town and city dwellers keep their cats entirely indoors without any problems. High-rise homes benefit from protective mesh over windows and balconies to prevent cats falling from them accidentally.

Cross-breed or pedigree?

You may have an idea of your ideal cat in terms of colour, type and temperament – one that looks pretty, is affectionate towards you and behaves perfectly in all respects. However, you must bear in mind that cats are living beings; each is an individual with its own character. You cannot, therefore, buy one 'off the shelf', ready-programmed to be the perfect pet you envisage. You can choose your preferred colour and type but, to a great extent, the way the cat behaves and relates to you will come down to the way you care for, handle and interact with him. Some pedigree cats are known for certain character traits, such as a laid-back attitude and a strong affection towards humans, and this can make the job of choosing a cat easier.

Types of cat

There are now more than 50 distinctive pedigree breeds and hundreds of colour varieties. All domestic cats, whatever their colour, coat length or temperament, fall into one of the three main groups – pedigree, cross-breed or non-pedigree.

1 Pedigree (pure-bred)

These cats are bred from pedigree parents of the same breed. The advantage of getting a pedigree is that you know what he will look like when he is fully grown and, providing you have checked out information about the breed, you will have a very good idea of his typical temperament and characteristics as an adult.

2 Cross-breed

Such cats are the offspring of pedigree parents, but of different breeds – for example a Persian crossed with a British Shorthair. The resulting kittens could grow

The 'Peke-faced' Persian is a desirable show cat, but 'typey' cats (those with exaggerated features) are prone to respiratory and other problems.

up to resemble either parent, or a mixture of both. Some could be longhaired, some shorthaired and others semi-longhaired.

3 Non-pedigree

Cats are described as non-pedigree if one or both parents were cross-bred themselves. Different breeds may have been mixed over generations, which can make the appearance, character and temperament of offspring difficult to predict.

Coat lengths

There are two types of coat: shorthair and longhair (the latter is often incorrectly referred to as 'Persian', which is a breed in its own right). Each is exactly as the name suggests, although some coats are thicker

TYPE	PROS	CONS
Pedigree	• Having researched the breed, you can pin-point your ideal pet, usually knowing what to expect in terms of appearance and character. • Many types and colours exist, appealing to individual tastes. • You can choose the type and colour you want, although you may have to wait a while for your exact requirement. • Pedigree cats are usually raised with the greatest of care, so you should expect a healthy animal.	• Pedigree cats are more expensive than cross-breeds. • Some breeds are prone to hereditary problems, or particular ailments (especially those bred to 'type'). • Some breeds have particular character traits, or care requirements, that may not be appealing you or practical for your lifestyle. • Certain breeds can be difficult to obtain as they are rare, or the demand exceeds availability.
Cross-breed	• Usually less expensive than pedigrees. • If you know what the parents are like, you have a fair idea of what to expect in terms of appearance and character. • Generally more hardy than pedigrees, but this does depend on the cross and the genetic parentage. • Because the crosses are usually intended, you can normally expect the resulting animals to be well socialized and healthy. Do be aware though that this is not always the case.	• They are not always readily available, especially if you want a very specific cross-breed. • Due to the character and behaviour traits of the breeds involved, certain combinations can be quite explosive, such as Burmese crossed with Siamese. Both breeds are attention-seeking types, highly active and vocal, so the two combined can result in an extremely demanding pet! Some owners may enjoy this, while others could find such an animal exhausting and infuriating.
Non-pedigree	• Free, or inexpensive. • Wide type and colour choice. • Usually easily available. • Generally uncomplicated in health terms.	• The character traits of the parents are generally unknown, so how the cat will mature in terms of looks, behaviour and character is hard to predict. • You may have to wait a while to find the age, colour and sex of your choice. • You cannot always be sure that the animal has been properly raised and cared for, so look out for signs of ill health and behaviour problems.

Siamese are affectionate and very sociable cats. If you are not going to be about during the day, it is best you get another cat to keep him company.

than others, depending on the breed of cat. A variation on the shorthair is the 'hairless' (such as the Sphynx), which has only a thin covering of down on the ears, muzzle, tail and on the external genitals of males. Semi-longhaired coats are not as thick, nor as long in some cases, as full longhairs. Some breeds have curly coats (Cornish Rex, Selkirk Rex and the La Perm, which can be either long- or shorthaired).

Coat colours

Cat coats come in many different colours, with the pedigrees boasting the most variations. The basic colours of the cat are simple to interpret – black, white, cream and silver, for instance – but others are more obscure colour such as blue-cream and colourpoint(see the chart right).

Appearance

Cats come in all shapes and sizes to suit all requirements and tastes. Examples include: the Munchkin with its short legs (said to be suitable as house pets because they are unable to jump onto kitchen worktops); the Scottish Fold which has folded ears; the American Curl with curled ears; the Manx which has no tail; the Japanese Bobtail which sports a short curly tail (called a pom); and the lynx-like American Bobtail with its unusual voice.

Your lifestyle

This determines, to a great extent, what sort of pet you should be looking for. In the cat's lifetime you are responsible for his health and mental well-being, and must find others to fulfil this role if you are unable to do so, for instance when you go on holiday or have to be away from home for any reason.

Some breeds are very high-maintenance compared with others, so only consider these types if you are able to provide properly for them for their life span. If you acquire a longhaired cat, you must be prepared to learn how to care for his coat properly; if you choose an extrovert, energetic type, then you must have the time to give him all the attention he needs. Such considerations may seem obvious, but

Bi-colour A white coat with dark patches.

Blue Any shade of cold-toned grey.

Blue-cream Dilute version of tortie with a mingled or patched coat of palest grey and cream. There are other colour varieties, including chocolate-cream, lilac-cream, and so on.

Bronze Warm coppery brown which lightens to buff.

Brown Any shade of dark brown – except in a brown tabby, when it refers to a cat that is genetically black and has black markings on an agouti (grizzled, like a wild rabbit) background.

Cameo White fur with red tips.

Caramel A subtle shade of pale orangey brown.

Champagne Buff-cream with warm honey beige shading to pale gold tan.

Blue

animal welfare organizations still have to cope with thousands of pet cats abandoned because their owners felt unable to care for them properly. Ultimately, picking a pedigree or non-pedigree cat is your decision.

You are in the best position to make an informed choice and, therefore, end up with a pet that is the right colour and type. How you will turn your chosen cat into the ideal companion you desire, given your lifestyle and expectations of him, is detailed in the following pages.

Cream

Chinchilla White coat with tips of a darker colour.

Chocolate A rich, warm brown.

Cinnamon Lighter shades of chocolate.

Colourpoint Self body with the tail, paws, mask (face) and ears of another colour.

Harlequin A bi-colour coat: 50–75 per cent white; 25–50 per cent colour.

Lilac Very pale, warm-toned grey.

Mink A range of colours in the Tonkinese breed.

Parti-colour Covers both bi-colours and torties.

Patched Two-tone tabby coat with darker and lighter patches, mingling tortie and tabby. Patched is sometimes also referred to as tortie – which can prove confusing.

Platinum Pale silvery grey with pale fawn undertones.

Red All shades of ginger. Deep coppery tones are the most sought after.

Ruddy A modification of black in the Abyssinian breed to reddish brown and burnt sienna.

Sable A term sometimes used to describe dark brown cats who are genetically black.

Self One colour.

Smoke White undercoat, topcoat hair white at the roots and coloured at the ends.

Sorrel Modification of red in the Abyssinian to brownish orange to light brown.

Tabby There are four basic patterns: ticked (each hair has contrasting dark and light colour bands); mackerel (vertically striped); spotted (as it suggests); and the classic (sides are blotched with whorls or 'oyster' marks).

Tipped Hairs are differently coloured only at the ends, which can create a sparkling effect.

Tortie-and-White (Calico) Tri-coloured (black, red and white).

Tortie (Tortoiseshell) A two-coloured (black and red) coat.

Blue, tortie and white

When and where to get a cat

Thinking about getting a cat and getting one can be two very different things. Whether you opt for an adult cat or a kitten, you must take into account your circumstances at the time. You may want a cat, but would a cat want to be with you right at this moment in your life?

Poor timing

The time is not ideal to get a cat if you are:
• moving house or due to go on holiday.
• busy at work and home or preparing for a large celebration.
• changing jobs or being made redundant.
• ill or expecting a new baby.
• separating from your partner or mourning a death.

Of course, there are exceptions to the rules, and many people find comfort in their pets at times of stress. However, animals feel their owners' anxieties and do worry. It is important, therefore, to ensure that you are in a position both materially and emotionally to offer a secure and harmonious home to a cat before you start to look for one.

Cat availability

Sometimes it is not as easy to get a cat as you might imagine:
• If you want a particular breed, colour or sex of cat or kitten, you may have to reserve your specific requirement with several breeders so that when such an animal becomes available you have first choice.
• Kittens are dependent on breeding seasons.
• Kittens tend to be in high demand at rescue centres, so you may have to wait until one becomes available.
• There may not be the exact type of cat you want at rescue centres immediately, so be prepared to wait.

Finding a cat

Your local paper, pet shops, vet surgery notice boards, cat magazines, word-of-mouth through friends and family and rescue centres are all potential sources of a cat or kitten. A kitten should be at least eight weeks old before it is safe for him to leave his mother. By this time, he should be weaned onto kitten food and be socialized with a wide range of people and animals. Some breeders prefer to wait until their kittens are 12 weeks old before homing, so that they are litter-trained and have had their initial vaccinations.

Which source is best?

No one source is best, as there are considerations to take into account with all of them.

Breeders

When obtaining a kitten from a breeder, try to select him from a whole litter if possible. The appearance of the young cats will influence your choice, but so too should their behaviour and health; it is better to pick one that appears healthy, outgoing, friendly and approaches you confidently. Avoid taking on a cat that looks unhealthy, since you may be taking on a problem.

Sometimes it is possible to get an older pedigree pet from a breeder who has no further need for a particular cat, or kittens resulting from accidental matings and not suited to a breeding programme.

Friends or family

An older cat can be a good idea if you do not have time to spend training a kitten, particularly if you are offered a well-behaved and friendly animal by a family member or a friend.

Animal rescue centre

If you decide to choose a pet from a rescue shelter, find out as much as you can from the staff about his background. Some cats, for example, may not be house-trained if they have spent their lives roaming about on their own and such animals may not integrate into a domestic environment.

Stray cats

Sometimes a cat simply moves into a home where he finds a welcome, or you may come across one you think has been abandoned. However, if you do find a 'stray', be aware that someone could be grieving over the disappearance of their pet, so make every effort to trace his owners by informing the local authorities and local rescue shelters, by putting up 'found' posters in local shops and veterinary clinics, and by having the animal checked for a microchip. Once you are satisfied that he is a stray, have him checked over by a vet to ensure he is healthy, and have him neutered if necessary.

Pet shops

Buying a cat from a pet shop can be risky, so be especially critical. Ensure that the animals in the store look well cared for, have adequate space, food and water, and appear healthy. If many cats are kept together in a less-than-ideal environment, and there is a constant turnover of 'stock', then there is a high risk of infection, which may not manifest until after you get your new pet home.

How much will a cat cost?

- Pedigree breeder – depending on the breed and whether or not the cat is of show quality, prices can vary enormously.
- Rescue centre – there is generally a charge to cover the cost of vaccinations and neutering.
- Stray – free.
- Pet store prices vary – pedigree cats are more expensive than non-pedigree.
- Friends or family – non-pedigree kittens or adult cats are generally free 'to good homes'; part-pedigree and pedigrees can vary, depending on the reason for rehoming.

A good option is if you know of a friend or neighbour whose cat has recently given birth and who is looking for homes for the kittens.

What you'll need

The vast array of equipment and products available designed for cats can be bewildering for a new or prospective owner. However, many of these items are simply not essential. As long as your cat is warm, has somewhere to rest comfortably, safely and undisturbed, is fed regularly, has a constant supply of fresh, clean water, has somewhere suitable to relieve himself, and has some toys to play with, he will be perfectly happy.

Food and water bowls

Your cat should have his own food and water bowls, placed on a spongeable feeding mat or a piece of newspaper to catch any spills.

Litter tray and cat litter

A litter tray is essential even if you allow your cat to go outside. There are two basic types – open and covered (hooded). Covered types prevent the litter being scattered outside the tray, contain smells better and afford the cat more privacy. However, some cats don't like to be enclosed so will only use an open tray.

Choose a tray big enough for your cat and one that will hold a good depth of litter – cats like to bury their waste completely, without wetting or soiling their paws. Lining the tray with newspaper will make cleaning it much easier. Place the tray on newspaper or a piece of vinyl floor covering, so spills will be easy to clean up. There is a wide variety of types of litter, which vary in cost, effectiveness and ability to reduce odours.

Litter types include (clockwise from the top) clay-based litter, fine-grain litter with a grit/sand-like consistency, and wood-based litter comprising sawdust or paper pellets.

Bed and bedding

There are many types of cat bed. Blankets, fleece material, a cushion or old pillow, and fleecy veterinary pet bedding all make good, insulating bedding material. What you buy will depend largely on appearance and cost. Wash bedding regularly to remove dirt and help prevent fleas.

Toys

Playing with your cat is rewarding for both of you. Cats play most during kittenhood, and if they learn to play with toys during

this time they will probably continue to do so during adulthood. Moving toys in ways that mimic prey will result in more fun for your cat and more interest for you. Darting movements from side to side in front of your cat, rather than up and down movements, are more likely to result in play. Toys that move erratically or very fast, then are stationary, are more likely to be 'hunted'. Many stuffed toys contain the herb catnip, which cats find irresistible.

Collar and identity tag

Ideally, your cat should wear a reflective or fluorescent collar complete with an identity tag and a bell to warn wildlife and birds of his presence. Collars come in many designs, but you should always use one with either an elastic insert or a quick-release fastening for safety, in case your cat becomes caught up on something.

Cat carrier

For trips to the vet or cattery, you will need a cat carrier. Choose one you find easy to handle and carry with the weight of your cat in it, with a secure door closure. There are various types:
• Cardboard – cheap and fine for occasional use, but will not contain a cat that is determined to get out, and are liable to break when wet.
• Fibreglass – front opening, draught-free, secure, light and easy to clean.
• Plastic-coated wire-mesh – top-opening and ideal for cats that dislike being enclosed too much.
• Wicker carriers – look nice, but are hard to clean and not hardwearing.

Cat flap

A cat flap fitted in an outside door or window will, when unlocked, allow your pet to enter and leave the house at leisure. Various designs are available, including

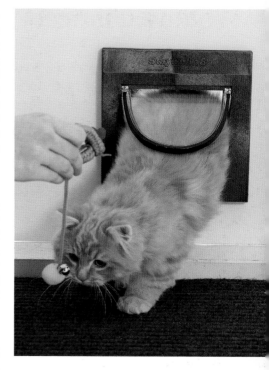

Some types of cat flap can be set into brick walls, which is handy if you don't want to put one in a door or window.

electromagnetic and electronically operated flaps that will only open to the cat carrying a special device attached to his collar. Fit the cat flap low enough in the door or window for your pet to be able to use it comfortably, and far enough away from the handle or fastening on the door or window to prevent burglars from reaching inside and letting themselves in.

Parasite treatments

You will need to treat your cat for internal and external parasites on a regular basis – the most effective treatments are only available from vets, but are worth spending a little bit more on as they work efficiently, unlike many shop-bought products.

Feeding your cat

Feeding your cat a well-balanced diet and the right amount of food on a daily basis is essential for his good health. There is a wide range of foods available for cats, so it can be difficult deciding which variety is best for your pet. There are, however, certain dietary nutrients that a cat cannot do without. Taking these and your cat's age, health and lifestyle into account when purchasing cat food can help to make the job of deciding which diet is most suitable easier.

Cats depend on meat and other similar foodstuffs, such as fish, as sources of vital nutrients in order to remain healthy. Unable to exist on a low-protein diet, cats need relatively large amounts of meat-based food per day in relation to their size. Do not feed your cat on dog food.

Necessary nutrients

It is important to ensure that the balance of nutrients fed to a cat is correct, as excesses can cause as many health problems as deficiencies. It is better to feed good commercial foods, rather than a home-made diet as this makes it is difficult to ensure your cat is receiving all the correct nutrients. For example, a diet of cooked meat alone is low in calcium, vitamin A and iodine, and these deficiencies may lead to osteoporosis. Conversely, a liver-rich diet can cause excess vitamin A, resulting in bony growths around the joints and spine that make movements painful.

Carbohydrates

Although they can digest cooked carbohydrates, cats do not need them, as their high-protein diet supplies all the energy they require. However, foods such as breakfast cereals can provide a useful source of energy.

Vitamins

A relatively high level of vitamin A is needed to keep body cells working properly. B vitamins are important for maintenance of the central nervous system. Vitamin D helps the body produce calcium, essential for healthy bones and teeth, although cats need far less than dogs or humans. Phosphorus is essential for healthy bones and teeth while vitamin E helps prevent cell damage. Vitamin C is not needed.

Proteins

Proteins in meat help build and repair body tissue and make hormones. They also supply essential amino acids.

To help ensure good health, kittens require more frequent feeding than adult cats, with up to five meals a day.

Fats

Dietary fats make a concentrated energy source and supply the essential fatty acids (EFAs) that are vital for total body health.

Fibre

A lack of fibre in the diet can result – especially in elderly, inactive cats – in constipation and other digestive problems. Sources of fibre include cooked vegetables and cereal foods.

Food types

Good quality proprietary foods are the easiest to feed. They contain the necessary nutrients in the correct proportions. There are three forms of ready-prepared food.
• Wet/moist (canned or pouch) Canned food has a high water content, is available in a wide range of flavours and is usually the preferred choice of cats.
• Semi-moist (pouch) Often containing vegetable protein, such as soya, this food type contains less water than canned, and keeps well in a bowl without drying out.
• Dry (packet) This contains minimal water, so your cat will need plenty of water with it. Its hard, crunchy texture helps keep cats' teeth tartar-free and in good condition. Use it as only part of the diet – some cats become addicted to it, and it can result in urinary problems.

Life-stage feeding

Different feeding regimes are appropriate for the various stages in a cat's life:
• From weaning (about 8 weeks) to 12 weeks – 5 small meals of kitten food a day, each of around 25 g (1 oz).
• From 12 to 20 weeks – 4 meals a day.
• From 20 to 30 weeks – 3 meals a day.
• From 30 weeks to 12 months – gradually reduce to 2 meals a day.
• From 12 months to 8 years – 1 or 2 meals a day.

Water is essential for life, and your cat should always have access to a fresh supply. Refill the water bowl each day and scrub it out regularly.

• From 8 years onwards – 1 or 2 meals a day, (or more depending on his health).
• Pregnant females – 2 or 3 meals a day, 240 g (8½ oz) in all

When to feed

Most owners feed either morning or evening – or both, depending on their cat's needs or preferences. Encourage him to eat his food at a single sitting rather than leaving uneaten food out all day. Wet food, in particular, goes off rapidly. You will soon get to know how much your pet will eat at one sitting.

Feline obesity is a common problem, so it is essential to restrict your pet's daily ration to the manufacturer's or your vet's guidelines. Treats should come from the daily ration allowance, not as extras.

Home-made food

Many cats appreciate 'home-made' foods, but basing an entirely balanced diet around these will be very difficult; a vitamin and mineral supplement will almost certainly be required as well – consult your vet for advice on what to give your cat.

The home environment

To be healthy, your cat must feel safe and secure in his environment and you need to be positive that you are doing all you can to keep him happy and protected from harm. Fulfilling your cat's natural needs will help keep you both contented.

Home comforts

To a cat, the most important thing is to mark his home with his own smell, which he does by rubbing his cheeks (where his scent glands are) on furniture and other items. Glands between the toes also leave a scent message as the cat strops his claws. Humans cannot smell this scent, but other cats can and know that he is there.

Surrounded by his own scent, a cat feels more secure, but over-zealous house cleaning with strong-smelling chemicals, can keep overriding this feline scent. This may make the cat anxious and lead to rigorous marking that may involve the cat spraying urine around the house.

High and mighty

Cats like to get high up to rest, so you can help to increase his feeling of security by providing high-up places where he can rest without being bothered.

Playtime

Cats tend to be at their most lively at dawn and dusk, as this is when prey is particularly vulnerable. While dusk is not usually a problem for owners, dawn can be. Establish other times when you can give your cat attention as part of his regular routine.

Interaction

Some cats will be more independent and aloof than their owners wish. Cats that

Stairs provide cats with a good opportunity to get up high if they are worried. There they can assess the situation and decide if what they perceived is actually a threat.

have a low need for social contact may learn to tolerate their owners' attention, but never really seem to enjoy it, so their desire to be left alone must be appreciated and accepted. Other cats (such as Siamese and Burmese) will actively seek human company and show signs of distress if they cannot get enough.

Harmony outside

If your cat has access to a safe outdoor environment, then he will have the best of both worlds – freedom to roam as nature intended and a warm bed and food to come home to. If you allow your cat out, you do need to consider your neighbours, his safety and the effect on the local wildlife.

For all of these reasons, it might be worth building a large outdoor pen with shelter. Your pet will then be safe and able to enjoy being outdoors, your neighbours will be happy and the local birds will also be safe.

Outdoor safety

• **Poisons** Keep chemicals, such as oil, antifreeze, weedkillers and pesticides, locked away. Most cats will avoid poisonous plants, but kittens can fall victim to them. Remove any dangerous plants – your vet can advise you. Cats can also suffer poisoning from eating contaminated prey animals and birds so clear carcases away.

• **Toad poisoning** Cats catch frogs, and the occasional toad, before they learn better. Toads emit a vile, toxic, substance when under threat. If you see your cat shaking his head frantically, salivating and pawing at his mouth, consult your vet immediately.

• **Snake bites** Consult your vet immediately if you suspect your cat has been bitten by a poisonous snake.

• **Drowning** Rainwater tanks can prove lethal to curious cats. Ensure the lids are secured and weighted down.

Indoor living

Urban living is becoming increasingly dangerous for cats, so many owners prefer to keep their cats inside. Boredom can be a major problem with indoor cats and often leads to behavioural problems. If an indoor routine is established correctly, then it can be successful, if you keep your pet stimulated, exercised and entertained.

Indoor safety

Although you think your home may be safer for your cat than the great outdoors, there are a number of potential hazards you need to be aware of for your pet's well-being.

• **Cookers or hobs** Cats will insist on jumping onto things, the cooker/hob being no exception, and they can burn their paws.

Always check under your car before driving off in it. Cats have a tendency to sit underneath stationary cars, and also, if they can climb in, to curl up under the bonnet of a parked car for warmth.

Keep him out of the kitchen while cooking, and make sure the cooker/hob has cooled down before letting him in.

• **Washing machines/tumble dryers/ freezers/refrigerators** Check these before closing the door.

• **Cleaning fluids and detergents** Make sure your cat does not have access to these.

• **Powder carpet fresheners** Cats may suffer paw, skin and respiratory problems from these products, so avoid them.

• **Electric leads** These can prove fatal if chewed. Keep wires to a minimum in areas of the house where cats are allowed

• **Sewing materials** Keep needles, thread, buttons and elastic bands safely away from your pet.

• **Human medicines** Keep these in a cupboard or drawer, so your cat does not have access to them.

• **Hot water** Keep your cat out of the bathroom while you are running a bath in case he jumps or falls into the hot water; run the cold water first and add the hot afterwards.

Bringing your cat home

Before you bring your new pet home, you must prepare for the big event so that it runs comfortably and smoothly and is stress-free for all concerned. Setting a date well in advance for when you will collect your cat will give you time to get ready all the things you will need.

When to collect your cat

Wait until you have time to spare (or take a week off work) before bringing your cat home, so that you are around to help him settle in. This is especially important if he is a kitten. Your task will be to keep him company, show him where his food, water and litter tray are (and house-train him if necessary) and introduce him to the rest of the household.

Set aside a room in which to keep the cat safe for a day or two while he settles down; prepare this with food and water bowls, a litter tray, bed and toys. Make sure the rest of the family know that he should not be disturbed while in this room to give him the chance to acclimatize.

If you don't have a spare room, put a pen in the quietest area of the house and use this as the 'sanctuary' for the first few days of the cat's arrival.

Pre-arrival preparations

A couple of days before you collect the cat, take the bedding he is to use to the breeder so he can use it there. His smell, or that of his mother and litter mates, will transfer to the bedding and make him feel more at home in his new environment. Take two lots of bedding, in case he has an 'accident' on the way home.

Buy the equipment you will need (see pages 18–19), in particular a sturdy cat carrier. Find out from the breeder or owner what food and cat litter the cat is used to, how much he is being fed, and how often.

At the collection point, line the carrier with the bedding, put the cat in and shut the door securely. Ensure you have all the paperwork from the former owner (receipt, pedigree papers, registration and ownership transfer documents and

When introducing yourself and children to the cat, sit on the floor so that you appear smaller and therefore less threatening to him.

Many cats position themselves away from the main action to observe the new environment and the people; don't try to prevent them from doing this, or haul them out of a place where they feel secure.

vaccination certificate). Also take a little of his used litter back home with you to transfer into his new litter tray.

Travelling home

Secure the carrier on a seat with a seat belt, in the back of an estate vehicle, or in the footwell. The inside of the vehicle should be of a moderate temperature with sufficient airflow so that the cat is comfortable; too much heat can be fatal on long journeys. Offer water in a pet drinking bottle at regular intervals if you are travelling any distance. Even if the cat protests at being in the carrier all the way home, do not be tempted to let him out. Talk to and reassure him, which may help him to settle.

On arrival home

Transfer the cat from the carrier straight into the room or pen. Take a few minutes to reassure him before closing the door and leaving him undisturbed for an hour or two to settle down. When you do let the cat out into the rest of the house, leave his room or pen door open so he can retreat to his sanctuary. Make sure children behave quietly and gently around him – do not let them handle him too much until he has got used to them. Allow the cat to investigate you and his new surroundings at his leisure; feeding him will help you establish a bond.

After this introduction, put the cat back in his sanctuary for his first night. See pages 37–39 for detailed information on socializing your new cat with people, other cats and other animals.

Settling in

Keep the cat in his room or pen for the first week (let him out for exercise and gradual acclimatization), and then you can allow him free access to the rest of the house. Feed and play with him at regular times to establish a routine that he looks forward to and so strengthen your relationship.

Do not let him outside for the first 2–3 weeks, depending on the cat's character, otherwise you risk not seeing him again. Friendly, laid-back cats are likely to adjust to their new homes more quickly than timid ones. Once the cat is feeling at home, you can move his bed and litter tray to their permanent positions, showing the cat where they are. You can also gradually introduce him to wearing a collar.

FELINE BEHAVIOUR

Cats have their own unique language. If we observe them carefully, however, we can build up a detailed picture of their body language and actions that helps us guess how they might be feeling, what they want from us and what they need. By making the effort to learn what your cat is saying to you, you will understand him better and therefore be able to give him a better life. Many cats are treated badly or inappropriately because their owners do not understand what their cat is telling them. As intelligent humans, it is our responsibility to learn about the language of the animal we keep as a pet.

Body language

Cats communicate with a wide range of facial expressions, vocal sounds and body postures. Many people talk to their cats, and sometimes they seem to understand each other. Cats have a considerable universal vocabulary and some people have tried to translate precisely what they are saying; you too can learn to recognize what your cat is communicating.

Friendly

Tail up and curled in greeting, and paw raised ready to come forward once he is sure it is safe to approach and rub against the person or other animal in an effort to make friends quickly.

Relaxed

With paws tucked under him, this cat has no fear that they will be needed. Hind legs are outstretched, and he is in a vulnerable position that a tense, wary cat would not adopt. Ears pricked and eyes wide open indicate that something has caught his interest.

Playful

This cat is relaxed and playing.

Anxious and worried

His tail is tucked under to keep it out of harm's way and his weight is centred over his hind legs in readiness to run or strike with his front claws. His ears and whiskers are rotated to keep them out of the way in a fight and his eyes are looking upwards, seeking a safer place higher up. He is miaowing loudly to attract a rescuer.

Stalking

This cat is completely motion-less, his eyes are wide open for maximum visual information and focusing on the prey. His ears are pricked for maximum sound information on the exact location of the prey, and his back end is bunched up ready to spring (wagging from side to side immediately before he executes the pounce).

Attention-seeking or hungry

If this Manx cat had a tail, he would raise it in greeting. His ears are pricked, his expression alert and he is standing tall on his paws in an effort to get nearer to a person's face for attention – either for petting or feeding. This posture is usually accompanied by the cat winding himself around legs, rubbing himself against a person and using vocal sounds (from strident miaows to 'chirrups') to gain his owner's ear.

Wary

Crouched down, back end low, tail tucked under and poised ready for flight, this cat is wary about what he has seen or sensed. His face is tense and watchful, and his ears pricked to pick up sound information.

Submissive

This kitten is crouching low to make himself as insignificant as poss-ible and is not retaliating, yet he is poised to make a quick getaway if necessary. His ears are back to keep them out of harm's way.

Behaviour in the home

What represents normal behaviour to a cat is instinctive. Some feline
actions and behaviours may puzzle owners, but it is important to
understand that they are done for a reason – primarily so that the cat
feels safe and sound in his home environment. No matter how tame
you may think your pet is, you have to remember that he is still
a wild animal at heart.

Hunting

A cat does not fully know
how to pursue and kill prey
through instinct alone; his
hunting technique develops through
learned behaviour as a kitten by watching
and imitating the actions of his mother. If a
kitten has not been taught these skills, he
may later on in life catch a prey animal, but
not know how to kill it. There are several
reasons why cats 'play' with their catches.

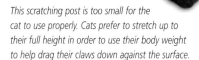

*This scratching post is too small for the
cat to use properly. Cats prefer to stretch up to
their full height in order to use their body weight
to help drag their claws down against the surface.*

• The cat is an inexperienced hunter, and
therefore a poor killer. He can catch the
prey but does not know how to finish it off.
• It is a way of weakening prey that may
otherwise bite its attacker in self-defence
before the cat puts his face close enough to
dispatch the victim.
• He may bring half-dead prey home for his
owner – viewed as a litter mate – to use for
practising hunting skills, in the same way as
a mother cat would bring it home for her
kittens to practise their hunting skills.

Obviously, pet cats do not need to hunt
for food, as their owners provide it for
them, but feral cats and wildcats do – hence
the need for them to retain the knowledge.
Undoing millions of years of evolution is
impossible and, apart from keeping your
cat indoors, or in a pen when outside, you
can do little to prevent him hunting.

Displaced hunting

Some cats, such as the Cymric, Ocicat and
Persian, have a stronger instinct to hunt
than others. If they are kept indoors, they
may turn their attention to other things that
move in the house, targeting adults,
children and other pets. Sometimes mock
chases and bites will comprise social play,
and in these cases the bites will be
inhibited; in other cases, cats will display
real predatory behaviour and, since this is
designed to catch and kill prey, considerable
damage can be done to the hapless victim.

Giving your cat the opportunity to go
hunting outside, or to play with and 'kill'
toys, can solve the problem. However, the
fact that cats will do this to members of the
family shows how deep-rooted their
hunting instinct is.

Sleeping

Cats spend a large proportion of their lives asleep. As predators, they do not need to spend a lot of time eating, so can afford to rest for much of the day. To conserve energy and reduce the time needed for hunting, cats prefer to sleep in warm, comfortable places. They like to nap rather than spend long periods of time asleep, but if relaxed enough to enter deep sleep they produce the same brainwave patterns as we do when we dream. During these moments their bodies twitch, so it is easy to conclude that they are dreaming about the day's activities, just as we do. If deprived of deep sleep over a long period, cats can become ill.

While asleep, a cat's hearing becomes even more acute than when awake, to provide warning of danger. When they fall asleep on your lap and then wake suddenly as if under attack from hands moving over them, most cats quickly realize that it is only their owner stroking them; but some react defensively and may scratch or bite in self-defence.

Stropping

Cats are armed with razor-sharp claws that are hooked at the ends so that they can get a good purchase on prey, and so that they can climb out of danger. Normally kept retracted so that they stay sharp, claws are protracted out of the flap of skin that covers them when the cat needs to use them to catch prey or climb.

Claws grow continuously and need to be kept trimmed and, periodically, the old outer casing needs to be removed to reveal the new, sharp claw underneath; this is done by scratching, or stropping, the claws down a suitable surface. Stropping is also done in strategic places in order to leave scent messages. In the garden, trees make good stropping sites, while indoors the furniture tends to be a favourite target – unless the cat is supplied with, and taught to use, a suitable stropping or scratching post.

Sitting in high-up places

Most members of the cat family use trees and other elevated places as vantage points for safety, eating and resting, and as hiding places from which to leap down and attack unsuspecting prey below. Cats are equipped with sharp, hooked claws that help them to run up most textured, vertical surfaces. Descent from high-up places is more difficult, as their claws give them little support, so cats will often back down in a hopping motion (rather like bears do) before turning and leaping to the ground.

Cats often watch birds through the window and perhaps go through some of the motions of catching them, and chatter their teeth at them as if frustrated that they cannot get to them.

Playing

Cats play with toys (and each other in some cases) for enjoyment and, more importantly, to develop their hunting and defensive skills or to keep them honed. Through play, kittens practise social, hunting and fighting skills to equip them for adult life. They learn to carry small toys, or prey victims their mother has brought them, in their mouths, and defend these from approaching siblings by growling and, if this does not deter them, striking out at them. As cats age, their desire to play and hunt slowly diminishes until they are content to sit around and doze for much of the time.

Urinating and defecating

When not leaving scent messages, cats like to bury their waste products. Digging a hole in which to deposit their waste, and then covering it up afterwards, ensures the area is kept clean and does not advertise their presence. Cats perform this action from an early age, as soon as they leave the nest, if an easily rakeable material is available to them. They prefer to use a substance of clean, dry consistency in which digging is easy, which is why sand or freshly dug earth are such favourites – much to the annoyance

This cat is relaxed and playing now, but when outside he is an efficient hunter. If he were positioning the 'prey' to deliver the killing bite he would be on top of it, pinning it to the ground.

of parents whose children have sandpits, and gardeners.

Cats like to hide when they are relieving themselves, and try to find a secluded place in which to do so where they will not be disturbed or vulnerable. It is important, therefore, to place litter trays in quiet places; if they are in a busy area, the cat may prefer to go behind furniture or another inaccessible place instead. Cats do not like using dirty, wet litter trays and will often go elsewhere rather than use them.

Scent messaging

A cat's sense of smell is highly developed. Cats use scent messaging to communicate at distance. Scent messages linger in the environment for some time, informing other cats and animals of the leaver's presence. As well as rubbing their facial and paw scent glands on surfaces, cats also use urine and faeces to mark their territory.

After investigating a scent message, a cat will then add his own to it. If the leaver is familiar without animosity, then a face-rub scent message is sufficient. However, if a stronger message is required the cat may choose to scratch or spray urine to cover the intruder's scent. In spraying and defecation scent messaging, cats can tell the messenger's age, sex, state of health and even what he ate recently.

Personal hygiene

Grooming fulfils many important functions in maintaining health. As well as keeping the coat and skin in healthy condition, straightening out the coat to make it a better insulator in cold weather and helping remove parasites, grooming can also cool a cat down in hot weather by spreading saliva on the fur. Cats also lick themselves dry if they get wet, as a wet coat does not provide the necessary insulation. Grooming also plays a part in relationships between cats, with the less important cat making an effort to groom the more confident one.

Exploring

To maintain physical and mental health, it is important for cats to know their territory well. This is so that they know the best sources of food, where potential enemies lurk and whether any intruders need warning off. Cats like to check their territory regularly and will investigate anything new.

Feline interaction

For cats who do not easily form friendships with others, coping with cats that are not part of their household but share their territory can be difficult. Disputes between cats over territory are common in overcrowded urban areas. One way of coping with this overcrowding is to 'time-share' the facilities, by leaving scent messages advertising the fact that part of the territory is temporarily occupied.

From these messages, and a knowledge of the felines in the area, a cat can tell how long ago the leaver passed by, who he was and whether it is safe to proceed – or whether it might be better to wait for a while, or go in another direction. Face-to-face encounters occasionally occur, but usually result in nothing more than lots of feline swearing and a standoff until the weaker cat backs down.

Hiding

Though armed with claws and teeth, cats are only small, so it makes sense for them to stay out of trouble when they can. Hiding when under threat is a good strategy. Domestic cats will often run and hide and keep still when they cannot get up high or run away from danger in the close confines of a house. Shy cats like igloo-style beds in which they can curl up and hide, therefore feeling secure.

A cat's instincts, even in their cosseted, domestic world, tell him that finding out his competitors for food and rivals for mates is vital for survival in the wild.

Territory

The ancestors of our domestic cats did not hunt in packs, but were solitary hunters who patrolled a territory that supplied them with the food they needed to survive. Although our pets are well fed by us and have no need to hunt, they have not lost the desire to stake out an area that they can call their own. To them, a territory represents safety and a food supply should their humans fail to provide for them.

Area

In an urban environment, a tomcat will opt for the largest territory he can lay claim to and defend, which may extend across several gardens; in country districts, this area may cover 1.5 square km (1 square mile) or more. House cats usually treat the home as a territory shared with their human household, with some core areas that are specific to themselves or others. They will accept that they are not allowed in certain places, at least if that territory owner is around, and may claim a particular chair or cushion as their own, unless forced off it by a more dominant member of the household.

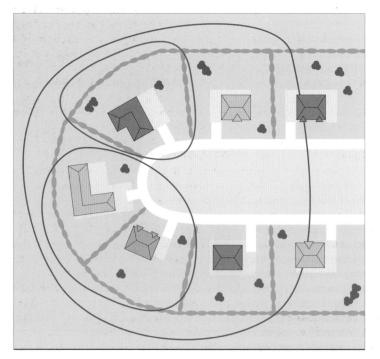

A schematic view of feline territories. Toms range over a wider area than females or neutered cats.

─── tom's territory

─── neutered cat's territory

─── female cat's territory

This cat is marking a bush as part of his territory by spraying a small quantity of urine onto it. He is standing as tall as he can, to aim the urine as high as possible, so that the message is at nose height and therefore impossible for other cats to ignore.

Outdoor cats lay claim to an area that they can defend from other households. This does not necessarily match human house and garden divisions and may include places not on the boundary with their house. A new arrival who finds his own backyard already claimed, and who is unable to drive off the occupant, may occupy somewhere several doors away.

In highly built-up areas where there are no gardens a cat may be reduced to an outdoor territory of little more than a rooftop or window ledge.

Marking

As well as using facial and paw scent messaging (see page 32), a cat will often use urine as a stronger form of messaging, and in laying claim to territory. Males generally spray droplets of strong-smelling urine onto every convenient object along the perimeters of their ranges. The tom examines a post or bush to see who has been along that way before, turns his back on it, raises his tail. Then, with two or three pedalling movements of his hind legs,

urinates high and accurately onto the object. Sometimes he will turn back to examine his signature, or back up and rub his tail and hindquarters against the damp patch; occasionally the tom will turn and smell his mark, then strop (scratch) his claws vigorously.

Female cats also sometimes develop the habit of spraying. Some adopt the typical male position and direct their urine backwards in a fine jet.

Territorial defence

If a cat receives a threat from another cat, or other animal, in its territory, the following happens.

• The cat freezes and looks at the intruder; his tail lifts and starts to flick slowly from side to side. His whiskers and ears point forward and his nose begins to quiver as he tries to identify the threat object.

• As the intruder moves closer, the cat changes his stance. The point of the lifted tail turns downwards, the chin is drawn in, and the ears flatten as the cat begins to turn slowly to one side. Gradually the back arches and the hairs on the cat's back and tail rise until he has assumed his aggressive posture in an attempt to scare the intruder off.

• This menacing display continues if the intruder continues to move forward. The cat faces the enemy but turns sideways to present as large and formidable an area as possible. The hind legs become tensed and ready to spring forward in attack or away in flight. He balances on one front paw, while the other is raised, claws unsheathed, ready to strike. He bares his teeth in a snarl.

• If the unwelcome visitor backs away, the aggressor may move forward slightly, smacking his lips and salivating, while continuing to growl.

• When the threat disappears, the cat sniffs the invaded ground and then marks it with his own scent.

If neither cat will give way and a fight ensues, it is often fast and furious with a great deal of noise; each cat tries to inflict as much damage on his rival as possible using both his teeth and claws.

When a cat adopts this hostile posture and hisses, it means that he is really worried about whatever he has seen or what is approaching him. Fluffing up the hairs on his body and arching his back makes him bigger, in an attempt to scare off the enemy.

In this territorial dispute, both cats are unwilling to back down. The cat standing on the fence is in a stronger position and may be the owner of the territory, which will give him added strength. Cats can sometimes hold positions like this for hours before one finally decides to withdraw.

Socializing

Integrating a new cat into a household is simpler if there are no other existing pets. If there are, then successful socialization is possible, providing you go about it the right way and are prepared to be patient.

Socializing with people

When you first get a cat, it is important that you let him come to you, rather than force yourself upon him. This is so that the cat does not feel threatened. The best way you can ingratiate yourself into your cat's affections is to feed him well and make sure he has comfortable, safe and warm places in which to rest.

Cats that have been well handled since birth, and brought up in a homely, friendly and laid-back atmosphere, tend to be more sociable and easily adaptable than those that have not. The amount of socialization a kitten has with people while he is two to seven weeks old determines how well he will interact with people later in life. Good experiences in a cat's early life help produce a friendly, outgoing cat.

Respecting your cat

Some cats enjoy the company of humans very much; others do not. Some cats are friendly for brief periods during the day, but spend the rest of the time on their own doing other things. It is a case of discovering what your cat prefers, and respecting that, in order to build and enjoy a harmonious relationship. If you require a high need for social contact with your cat, choose a breed or type that demonstrates this.

Some cats stay away from humans because of a lack of trust due to poor socialization during kittenhood. These cats are timid but can usually be slowly encouraged to be more friendly, and therefore more affectionate, through patience and gentle treatment.

Children, often unintentionally, can be a great source of discomfort to cats. They can be too noisy, too rough, too active, sometimes cruel – and altogether too much for a cat to cope with. For this reason, it is important to educate your children to respect pets and treat them as they would wish to be treated themselves.

How you physically handle your cat also has a great bearing on how he reacts to you. For detailed handling and interaction information, see pages 50–51.

Getting to know and trust human and animal members of the household will take a while, so be prepared to let your cat approach them first

A pen is the safest method of introducing two cats; alternate which one is placed in the pen over several introduction sessions.

Integration with other animals

Most cats, especially kittens, will integrate well with other animals in the household (as long as they themselves are well socialized), given a little time. When you bring a new cat home, it may help the introduction and socialization process to go smoothly if you transfer your existing pets' scent onto him. Do this by rubbing the cat with bedding from the pets' beds, or try taking smears from facial scent glands, before introducing them all.

Keep other pets away from the new arrival for the first hour or so, and then introduce them with either one or the other safely enclosed in a pen. Don't let dogs behave excitedly or bark around the new cat, or this will frighten him and get them off to a bad start. Usually, if he is well balanced and socialized with other animals, a dog will lose interest in the new cat – especially if you provide him with a toy or treat to take his mind off the new arrival.

Socializing with other cats

Introducing a cat to another cat may need to be a more gradual process, as they are not naturally sociable with unfamiliar members of the same species. Always supervise the initial meetings and

Given time and correct introduction procedures, even the most unlikely animals can become friends.

never try to force cats of any ages together – they will adjust to each other at their own pace. When they meet, the behaviour displayed by both parties depends on several factors:

• the age of the new arrival.
• the sex of the new arrival.
• the personality of the new arrival.
• the personality of the resident cat.

When meeting for the first time, a kitten and a resident cat will probably investigate each other nose to nose (which is why, no matter what age the cats are, it is safer for one to be penned so no harm can come to either). Depending on the kitten's personality, he may become frightened and back away, or show some bravado and even hiss; the older cat may ignore this behaviour and simply sniff at the kitten, or he may become threatening, in which case you may need to intervene. If all goes well, however, the cats will soon grow bored with each other and tolerate their presence without ongoing animosity.

In one interesting case, a newly arrived female kitten simply would not take the existing older cat's vocal threats and indifference for an answer – she was a confident youngster who wanted to play and she pestered the older cat until she got what she wanted. The two eventually became firm friends. In fact, when the kitten matured and had kittens of her own, the other cat (a neutered female) took it upon herself to act as midwife and then nanny to her friend's offspring.

If the new arrival is of the opposite sex, or both cats are neutered, then introductions can be easier. However, the personalities of the cats concerned play a large part in integration, and since this is something you cannot change – you simply have to work with and around them, taking into account each individual's needs and preferences.

This cat is totally relaxed and comfortable in his environment, so much so that he feels safe to lie in a vulnerable position while the family dog is in close proximity.

Give it time

Ensure that established pets get plenty of attention, so that they do not feel their security and status within the house is threatened by the new arrival. Having their own safe places to retreat to, undisturbed, when they feel the need, makes life easier for all concerned. It may take a week or two for the existing cat to accept the new arrival – longer if the new cat is an adult – but eventually things should settle down amicably. (See pages 40–41 for more information on introducing a second cat.)

Should I get a second cat?

Many owners decide to get another cat or kitten to provide their existing pet with a friend and company when they are not there. While the concept may be ideal, the reality is often not – with the resident cat being less than pleased with his new playmate. Being generally solitary creatures, most cats don't require a companion, so is it yourself you really want to indulge?

Will I be able to cope?

Before going ahead and getting another cat, ask yourself the following questions. If you can answer 'yes' to them all, then it is safe to go ahead.

• Have you got the time available to help the cats integrate?

• Can you cope with the inevitable routine upheaval of integration?

• Can you afford another cat? (Think of the extra food, vet and cattery bills.)

• Do you have the space and the facilities?

• Have you got the time available to care for two cats?

• Could you deal practically and patiently with behaviour problems that might arise?

Introducing a second cat

It is true that cats provide company for each other when you are not around to give them any attention, but only once they are accustomed to each other. Introducing a resident cat to a newcomer is not always as easy as it sounds. Some breeds, such as Korats and Ocicats, for example, do not tolerate other cats at all well.

Introducing another cat, or any other animal for that matter, once your pet has

Once cats get to know and are comfortable with each other, play-fights enable them to maintain their relationship and to learn about each other's abilities and strengths.

DO	DON'T
• Follow the advice given in 'Socializing' on pages 37–39.	• Suddenly ignore the resident cat in preference to the new arrival, otherwise the former will feel insecure while the latter may be forced into a jealous confrontation brought on by your attention.
• Expect integration to take quite some time.	
• Integrate the cats gradually, preferably with one in a pen to prevent either getting injured and to give them both a sense of security.	• Put them together and leave them to 'sort themselves out'.
• Allow them to investigate each other at their own pace.	• Leave the cats alone together before the hissing and spitting stage has ended. Only after this is it reasonably safe to allow them to intermingle when you are not around.
• When you feel they are ready to intermingle freely, wait until feeding time (when they are both hungry), place them in a room that has 'safety' places which either can retreat to if necessary, close the door and put down bowls of extra tasty food, well apart, then bring the cats in to eat. Stay with them while they feed to interrupt any antagonistic behaviour (dropping a big bunch of keys is a good distraction). Eating together in this way can help promote successful integration.	• Expect the cats to become buddies overnight. Despite your best intentions, some cats never become great friends and only just tolerate living with each other.
• Give the cats separate litter trays.	

There may be a certain amount of spitting and hissing when the cats are introduced and get used to each other but, providing they each have a safe area they can retire to when required, this antisocial behaviour usually abates.

become established in the household can often cause more problems than it solves, whereas two cats brought up together may well become inseparable friends. This being the case, it is better to get two cats at the start. This could be either kittens of the same age or from the same litter, or two cats that have been used to living with each other. This ideal cannot always be achieved, however, so it is essential to take into account normal feline behaviour, and learn to understand it – then you will be in a more informed position to initiate introducing another cat into the household with minimal stress to all concerned (See pages 42–45).

Cats do not live by the same code of conduct that humans do, so, instead of smiling and shaking hands on first meeting, they are more likely to swear at each other and then have a punch-up. As this would not start the relationship off well, it is important to follow the dos and don'ts listed above and not to let this situation occur.

Behaviour problems

Sometimes, pet cats can display what we consider to be behaviour problems. To the cat, however, such behaviour represents a perfectly normal action in the circumstances. It is up to us to try to understand why these problems occur and then rectify the situation so that the inappropriate behaviour can be cured, or redirected into an acceptable one.

Why cats behave strangely

In view of the constraints and relatively abnormal conditions under which pet cats live, it is surprising how few revolt against domestication or exhibit strange behaviour

patterns, but shock and trauma can produce disorders. Rough, unkind handling can result in a totally unbalanced and unpredictable cat, and any form of severe shock may result in reactions that induce collapse of the cranial nerve and death. This can also happen to over-humanized cats on whom care and love have been lavished; here the attack is as a result of the over-stimulation of the nervous system.

Drug and food additives can also cause unusual behaviour in cats, so these are another area to investigate if your pet behaves abnormally; changing a brand of cat food, or being on a course of medication can sometimes bring about character changes. Introducing a new pet or human baby to the household can cause fear in some cases and antisocial behaviour in others, so great care must be taken in effecting introductions (see pages 37–39 and 40–41).

Scratching furniture

The arms of sofas and chairs make great scratching posts as far as a cat is concerned, while curtains are great fun to run up and hide in; they are not to know that this behaviour is unacceptable to their owners.

Furniture scratching is a behaviour trait that owners probably view as the most infuriating, yet it can be one of the simplest to prevent.

Only a small amount of urine is sprayed when a cat marks, compared with the large volume that is expelled when cats squat to urinate.

Provide your pet with alternative scratching areas and hiding places, such as:
• a sturdy scratching post, either home-made or shop-bought (rub catnip on it to encourage your cat to use it) – if your cat likes to climb, choose a multi-purpose. play/scratching post or play centre
• cardboard boxes in which to hide.
• lots of toys to play with.
• if necessary, keep your cat out of the room(s) containing prized furniture and soft furnishings to prevent him marking or damaging them.

Urinating or defecating in the house

It is important to identify whether the behaviour comprises 'marking' or is simply inappropriate toilet behaviour. The latter may arise because:
• the cat does not like where his litter tray is positioned – maybe it is too close to his feeding or sleeping area.
• the tray is too small to accommodate the cat comfortably.

• the litter that is provided is unacceptable; for example, some cats prefer wood pellets to anything else.
• the tray is not cleaned out regularly enough.

Inappropriate toilet behaviour is relatively easy to cure, but marking can be more difficult as the cause of it may not be readily identifiable. When a cat marks or defecates in inappropriate places in the house, it is an indication that he does not feel secure within his territory, and may even feel threatened. Leaving waste deposits in prominent places around the house is a way of marking the territory as his own, thereby warning off perceived intruders – such as other cats, animals or people in the household.

In one interesting case, one married owner could not understand why her previously clean cat started to mark and defecate on the bed. It later transpired that her husband had been having an affair; when he moved out of the marital home,

the marking behaviour stopped and the cat reverted to using his litter tray as before. The wife deduced that the cat was objecting to, or feeling threatened by, the scent of the other woman on her husband!

To help make your cat feel more secure and comfortable within the home, see pages 16–17 and 22–23.

Straying and fighting

Unneutered cats, on reaching maturity, will make every effort to escape from the house and find a mate. If they are not allowed to do so, their frustration can lead to all sorts of behavioural problems, including constant attention-seeking, soiling around the home, aggression and incessant vocal

Sometimes cats can be encouraged to stray by kindly neighbours who make a fuss of the cat and feed him.

expression. Straying can become a real problem for owners who have unneutered male (tom) cats, while those with unneutered females may find they have toms hanging around the house and garden when their pet is in season. Straying can also lead to health problems – caused by fighting (see pages 35–40) and by contracting diseases and becoming injured – that can prove very costly in terms of emotional upset for the owner and the expense of necessary veterinary treatment.

Some cats panic and react defensively when touched on sensitive parts of the body such as the head, underbelly and legs. 'Attack' on these areas can trigger an aggressive biting and scratching response which is designed to get rid of the hand.

Biting and scratching

Pet cats rarely become aggressive unless they are being teased or ill treated. However, sometimes a cat reacts violently to being touched because he has been frightened when woken up suddenly, or is reacting to another threat: he may be watching a menacing dog or a noisy vacuum cleaner when his owner tries to pick him up, and thinks he is being attacked by the cause of his fear. Some cats also react defensively when touched on sensitive parts of the body. This behaviour is an understandable response created by the cat's complex defence mechanism.

Sexual disorders sometimes manifest themselves in pet cats when they are not neutered and become frustrated. Neutering usually brings about a marked improvement in behaviour and general health.

Separation anxiety

Some cats – particularly certain breeds, such as the Siamese and Burmese – have a high need for contact with their owners, and can become quite distressed if left alone for any length of time. This anxiety can result in various kinds of inappropriate behaviour being displayed, such as destructiveness or soiling around the house, and even obsessive tendencies such as self-mutilation and cloth- or wool-sucking.

Curing these habits can be difficult, since the answer lies in reducing the cat's feelings of anxiety; for example, if you are out at work all day and the cat reacts badly to being left alone, then there are a number of options to consider.

• Impregnate a soft toy with catnip for the cat to play with and cuddle up to for a feeling of security – some cats even respond well to a radio left on at low volume.

• Employ a petsitter.

• Put the cat in a cattery each day so he has company.

• Try to work from home as much as you possibly can.

• Rehome the cat with someone who is at home all day.

• Get another cat to keep him company.

If you ignore the attention-seeking cat, he will usually get bored and go and find something else with which to occupy himself.

All of these options to deal with separation anxiety have their drawbacks, and it very much depends on your circumstances and the cat's personality as to which one will work satisfactorily – it may be a process of elimination to find out which option will work best for you and your cat.

Attention-seeking

Cats that seek attention soon learn what patterns of behaviour result in their owners taking notice of them. Some knock objects over or off table tops or shelves, knowing that this will bring their owners rushing to see what is wrong; others miaow, rub around the owners' legs and reach up with their paws. Reading a newspaper can result in the cat playing with it, or lying on it to focus the owner's attention on the cat and not the paper.

The best way to deal with this behaviour, depending on the character of the cat, is to:
• provide him with something else to focus on, such as toys.
• move breakables out of his reach.
• make the cat's environment more. entertaining and therefore more stimulating for him (see pages 22–23).
• get into a routine of giving your cat attention at certain times of the day that are convenient to you, so that he gets his quota of quality time with you, and vice versa; this will keep you both happy.

Excessive self-grooming

Cats who are extremely bored or badly reared may indulge in excessive self-grooming. They lick and groom their bodies until some areas are raw, and may even suck at their paws, tail or rear nipples, purring and kneading, regressing mentally into kittenhood.

Eating or sucking cloth

This behaviour (which is similar to that of a young child who will suck on a dummy or snuggle up to a particular blanket for comfort) appears to be related to self-sucking. It sometimes occurs in otherwise well-balanced cats, especially in some strains of Siamese.

It is probably easiest to accept this habit and let the cat have his own piece of cloth to suck at. However, if the attraction is for man-made fibres and the cat swallows large amounts of the material, it could become impacted in the stomach and intestines and need removing surgically.

Providing your cat with places to explore will help keep him pleasantly occupied and, therefore, happy.

Finding toys that your cat likes to play with by himself will help to alleviate any boredom during the times when you are not available to give him attention.

CARING FOR A CAT

There are many aspects to cat care and management, and part of the attraction of owning these splendid creatures is the interaction many owners enjoy in keeping their pets healthy and happy. There is something extremely satisfying in knowing that the animal in your care is receiving meticulous attention to all his needs. For many people, the daily routine in looking after a cat, from cleaning out his litter tray to making sure his coat remains tangle-free and glossy, is very fulfilling, and the purring affection received in return is blissfully comforting.

Handling cats

How you handle and interact with your cat will determine his behaviour and reactions towards you. Cats feel threatened and insecure when there is tension in the air, when they hear loud or raised voices, when they are touched roughly, and when they are suddenly grabbed at.

Picking up your cat

The best way to pick up your kitten or cat is shown here. Gently scoop him up with one hand under his chest, the other hand supporting his bottom, and keeping him close to your body so he feels secure. Don't hold him too tight, or he will feel claustrophobic and try to escape.

Carry the cat with your hand underneath his chest, your fingers between his fore legs, and keeping him close to your body for support. This leaves one hand free to hold the cat's head, or gently restrain him by the scruff (the loose skin on the back of the neck) if necessary.

Some people find it easier to hold the cat across his midriff, with one hand cradling the cat and the other hand held lightly across the length of his back for security (some cats also prefer this method of holding and carrying).

Looking at your cat's expression can tell you a lot about how he is feeling. Apprehension and worry show in this cat's face. His ears have swivelled back to find out what is going on behind him, and are held slightly back, indicating his concern.

Stroking

If stroked from an early age, most cats will be used to and enjoy it. However, there are areas on their body where stroking can cause them to worry. If the cat was not well handled as a kitten, or has been badly treated or teased, then it is wise only to stroke 'safe' areas – the back and sides. Avoid stroking the head where all the sense organs are, the sensitive tummy and delicate legs.

Cats often enjoy being stroked at the base of their tails, and will arch their backs in delight when you do this. Scent glands are situated in this area, and the cat appreciates any action that helps spread his own scent onto his companion. However, it is safer not to stroke the base of the tail unless you know the cat very well, as some cats may react defensively if they have had their tail pulled in the past by cruel humans, or if their tail has suffered injury at some time. If your cat scratches and bites you when you attempt to stroke or hug him, see pages 42–47.

You may dream of having a cat curled up on your lap, but consider your lifestyle before deciding to buy one. It's better to wait for the right time than cause unhappiness in the home.

Cats and children

Research has shown that children who grow up with pets in the house, and who are taught to treat them with respect and care, are more likely to develop into well-balanced and responsible adults. What better reason could there be to have a cat if you are a parent?

How cats view children

It is surprising just how tolerant some cats and kittens can be with babies and young children, but this is not something you should put to the test. You must teach children not to disturb the cat – especially by grabbing at him – when he is resting in his bed, or they may be rewarded with a scratch. Your cat may sleep for up to two-thirds of the day, which is quite normal.

Interaction

Discourage young children from picking up kittens and cats, because they may squeeze them too hard around the abdomen and put them off being carried for life. Instead, encourage the cat to climb on the child's lap and remain there to be petted. Show children how to stroke the cat, and also how to pick him up and carry him (see page 50). The cat should never be restrained during these encounters; make sure that the child understands that he or she must allow the cat to walk away whenever he wishes.

Prevent all children, especially toddlers, from chasing the cat, as this can put him off young children for life. Similarly, the cat should be able to rest undisturbed without being pestered, as nervousness and fearful or unpredictable behaviour are fuelled by lack of sleep. Provide plenty of areas to which the cat can escape from children's attentions – high-up places are preferable, so that your pet can seek sanctuary when it all gets too much for him.

If the initial interaction between children and cats is done correctly, most children and cats become great friends. Many cats and kittens bond quickly with children and seem happy to play with them, curl up with them to sleep or watch TV, and 'help' them with their homework.

Hygiene

Young children especially tend to put their hands in their mouths at every opportunity so, while it is rare that a child will pick up any infection (such as ringworm, tapeworm and toxoplasmosis) from felines, it goes without saying that you should take great care to ensure that children wash their hands after handling a cat (and other animals and pets) to minimize any risk. This is especially important if you have a garden that both cats and children like to use; cats will relieve themselves in flowerbeds and, if they get the chance, in sandpits – exactly where children like to play. Keep sandpits covered when not in use to prevent the cat using them as a toilet.

Toxoplasmosis

Contracting toxoplasmosis can be a great concern to expectant mothers, and those with children. Most infections are harmless if the person concerned has got sufficient immunity against them – which is why unborn and young children are at high risk.

Toxoplasma gondii is a microscopic parasitic that can cause abnormalities in the

foetus and blindness. Cats become infected by eating raw meat (via prey), and the resulting eggs (contained in cysts) from the parasite are shed in the faeces. These eggs hatch into larvae, and it is these that can cause the damage if ingested by humans. The toxoplasmosis parasite is also found in raw meats – primarily pork and chicken – in the human food chain, but is usually destroyed by cooking.

Some doctors and midwives can be over-zealous in advising expectant mums to get rid of any cats in the household to prevent any risk of contracting the disease, but this really is not necessary providing you follow hygiene rules and wear gloves when handling cats and cleaning out litter trays (or getting someone else to do it), and also when handling soil in the garden. The risks to humans of contracting toxoplasmosis are said to be greatest when handling raw

Children can sometimes find it hard to express their feelings to parents, or anyone else, for that matter. A cat, on the other hand, will not judge them or admonish them and, therefore, can be a source of great solace and friendship.

meat and vegetables grown in contaminated soil, or eating undercooked meat, so this puts the chances of contracting it from your cat into context.

If you are concerned about the risks, ask your doctor to carry out a blood test to show whether you are immune to the infection; if you are, this means that there is no risk of you passing it on to the foetus. If you are not immune, then make stringent hygiene practice in your kitchen and around your cat a priority. Ensuring your cat is wormed regularly is also good practice to keep the risk of contracting toxoplasmosis to a minimum.

Routine care

Cats look after themselves, don't they? Yes, to a certain extent they do, but for domestic pets to live happy, fulfilled and healthy lives they do need some help from their owners. In order to maintain your cat's mental and physical health, there are certain procedures you must implement on a daily, monthly and yearly basis.

Body condition

Pet cats can suffer from obesity if they do not get enough exercise in relation to the food they receive on a daily basis. Being overweight can result in serious health problems, and shorten the cat's life. Longhaired cats may look 'fat', but it can be an optical illusion created by all that fur. Depending on the breed or type, the average cat weighs around 4 kg (8 lb 12 oz), and you should be able to feel his ribs but not see them. Any deviation from normal weight may indicate a health problem.

Collars

If your cat wears a collar, check its fit daily to ensure it is not too tight, and is not rubbing, or in the case of flea collars, causing allergic skin reactions. Kittens grow rapidly, so it is especially important to check the fit of at least once a week.

Eliminations

The most important signs of a potential problem are:
- discomfort in urinating or defecating.
- a constant need to eliminate (shown by the cat frequenting his litter tray, often with no satisfactory result).
- blood in the faeces or urine, or other abnormalities, such as loose or very hard motions.
- not as many eliminations as usual.
  - any deviation from usual elimination – you should closely monitor this, and if it persists for more than a day seek veterinary advice.

General demeanour

If you know your cat well, you will soon notice any difference in his behaviour and demeanour. If he is normally bright and active, but suddenly appears depressed, this may indicate he is feeling unwell. If there are other signs of illness, then it is wise to take him to the vet for a check-up. Make a note of symptoms

Check regularly that your cat's collar and harness are neither too tight nor too loose.

as this may help the vet work out what is wrong. If your cat deviates from his usual eating habits, this also warrants investigation. He may simply not appreciate a change of food brand or, more seriously, he may be suffering from a mouth ailment or a digestive disorder that is affecting his appetite.

Training

Be sure to maintain rules about what the cat can and cannot do on a daily basis, so that you don't confuse him. If, for example, you don't allow him to scratch furniture, don't dangle toys over the arm of a chair, as this may lead to him digging his claws in the material, which in turn may encourage him to strop. If you don't usually allow the cat on the bed, don't be tempted to let him 'as a special treat' one day, otherwise the cat will then think he is allowed to be there all the time. Make sure the rest of the family also adhere to these rules.

Special occasions

At times when celebrations occur, cats need extra-special care to ensure they don't become stressed with all the noise and extra people in the house, or ill through eating anything unsuitable for them. Christmas trees, for example, can prove irresistible to curious cats, so make sure trees are well secured in their stands, lights are plugged into a circuit breaker, and decorations are shatterproof. Some cats can be fascinated by tinsel; if your pet persists in trying to eat it, you will have no option but to remove it from the tree.

Keep the cat separated from any celebrations by settling him in a quiet

Check your cat's eliminations on a daily basis to see what state his digestion system is in; loose motions can indicate a problem, as does a constant need to urinate.

room with a warm bed, some toys to keep him occupied, his litter tray, food and water; go in to check on him from time to time to reassure him that you are around. Even though you may be tempted to, do not give your pet foods that he does not normally receive, otherwise he may suffer unpleasant and painful digestive upsets.

The use of fireworks seems to be on the increase, and most animals are terrified of them. If they are going off in the neighbourhood, keep your cat safely indoors – having the TV or radio on can help drown out the noise which animals find distressing. If you do plan to host a fireworks party, ensure the cat is kept inside, preferably in a room on the other side of the house, and choose the 'silent' fireworks that you can now buy. It is also courteous to inform your neighbours of a forthcoming fireworks party, so that they can keep their pets safely inside when it occurs.

AT-A-GLANCE MAINTENANCE CHECKS

FREQUENCY	WHAT TO DO
Daily	• Clean food and water bowls. • Feed and supply fresh water. • Check eating habits. • Clean out litter trays and check for abnormalities in eliminations. • Give your cat some quality time – attention and play. • Check your cat is warm enough, depending on his age and the time of year. • Groom longhaired cats. • Check collar fit. • Check body, legs and paws for signs of injury.
Weekly	• Groom shorthaired cats. • Check ears. • General check for elderly cats – vital signs. • Check litter and food stocks for the forthcoming week. • Wash and disinfect litter trays; totally replace litter. • Check for weight loss or gain.
Monthly	• Parasite control – worm and deflea cats that have access to outside (see page 138 for more information). • General health check – vital signs.
Every two months	• Parasite control for indoor cats (do this monthly if you also have a dog that is allowed access to the outside). • Check and clean teeth (see pages 67 and 107–108 for more information on this subject, and ask your local veterinary practice staff for advice.).
Every six months	• If you choose injections to control fleas, they need to be administered every six months. • Veterinary check-up for elderly cats. • Vaccination booster injections for outdoor cats in highly feline-populated areas (see page 89).
Once a year	• Veterinary check-up (see page 61). • Revise nutrition needs depending on your cat's age (ask your vet for advice if necessary). • Yearly vaccination boosters injections.

If you take the time to learn what represents normal behaviour for your cat, you will soon be able to tell when he is feeling ill, or is displaying signs that something is not right and requires investigation.

Kitten care

You need to put in some work for that cute kitten to grow up into the perfect pet. It is not hard to do this – common sense, inclination and the will to apply certain principles and procedures into training your young cat how to behave as you wish him to will earn rewards.

Sleeping

Cats sleep for up to 60 per cent of their lives. They spend a larger proportion of their time asleep when they are kittens, and again when they reach old age. It is normal for kittens to sleep a great deal; because of their bursts of frenetic play, during which they use a lot of energy, they need to replenish their energy levels frequently through resting. It is essential that kittens are allowed to rest undisturbed as and when they wish, to make sure they have the necessary energy to develop into healthy, well-adjusted adults.

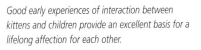

Good early experiences of interaction between kittens and children provide an excellent basis for a lifelong affection for each other.

Feeding

Kittens play hard and grow fast, and so require appropriate nutrition to cope with these demands on their bodies. Luckily for owners, manufacturers make this easy by providing a vast range of food especially formulated for young cats. Choose food for the appropriate life stage to ensure you are fulfilling your pet's nutritional needs. See pages 20–21 for further information on feeding kittens.

Juvenile behaviour

After sleeping and eating, playing rates highly in a kitten's priorities. He will amuse himself for hours with a selection of toys.

These do not need to be expensive, shop-bought ones for your kitten to have maximum fun: ping-pong balls, cardboard tubes and old soft and cuddly toys will do the job just as well. Make sure, though, that none of the toy items can break or come apart easily, as inquisitive kittens will soon chew off and swallow a teddy's button eyes, or dangling string, which could result in a tummy upset requiring veterinary attention, even surgery.

You can both enjoy hours of amusement simply by dragging a length of string along the ground for your kitten to chase, pounce on, and 'kill'. Never leave balls of wool or

Handling your kitten

The way in which you physically interact with your kitten will have a great bearing on how he reacts to you and other people when he matures. The better you handle your pet as a kitten, the better he will accept physical contact as an adult. For this reason, aim to give your kitten an all-over check at least once a week, but preferably every day.

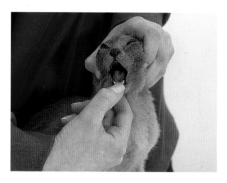

Accustoming your kitten to regular inspections of his mouth will reap dividends when you come to clean his teeth, and also when checking his mouth later on; your vet will also appreciate this training. In addition, it will make it easier for you to administer medicines orally.

Accustoming your kitten to handling and being touched all over will make being examined by a vet less stressful for him.

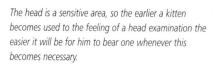

The head is a sensitive area, so the earlier a kitten becomes used to the feeling of a head examination the easier it will be for him to bear one whenever this becomes necessary.

Ears are sensitive, and therefore you should touch and handle them accordingly. Getting your kitten used to ear inspections will make life easier for both of you later on, should he ever need treatment for ear mites or a build-up of wax.

lengths of string unattended with a kitten, however, for the reasons given above.

Fishing rod-style toys, again, should only be used when you are there to supervise their use; cats risk strangling themselves by being allowed access to these play items when their owners are not around to supervise.

Praise, reward and punishment

Cats love praise and appreciate rewards, but they do not understand punishment as humans do; therefore they cannot respond to physical or verbal reprimands in the same way that humans might. For this reason, you must praise and reward any desired behaviour. Your kitten will soon learn that certain behaviour produces good things, and will therefore strive to attain these, whereas other types of behaviour produce no satisfactory response on your part, and therefore are unrewarding for him. If your kitten displays any kind of undesired behaviour, try to convert it into something more desirable (see pages 42–47).

Never physically reprimand your kitten, as this will not do any good; it will only serve to frighten him and alienate him from you. Remember that

building trust takes a good deal of time, but destroying it can only take a second of inappropriate response on your part.

Behaviour training

Start as you mean to go on. Instilling desired behaviour traits in a kitten will usually result in a sociable and well-behaved cat, bearing in mind the praise, reward and punishment ideals described above. For example, if you let your kitten sleep on your bed, then he will naturally expect to do so as an adult. So think ahead – behaviour you may find acceptable in a kitten may not be quite as desirable in an adult cat, yet the cat will not understand why you have changed your response. If you don't wish your cat to sleep on your bed as an adult, don't let him do so as a kitten and therefore come to expect this as the norm; denying him access to your bed later on may result in behavioural problems.

For many owners, training a kitten to perform a range of basic, acceptable actions by means of kind, gentle and effective methods is a mutually rewarding exercise. It really does help to be open to the feline view of the world to be able to communicate effectively (see pages 28–33).

Litter-training

Usually, a kitten will be litter-trained when ready for rehoming. However, once in his new home you will need to show him where his new toilet facilities are. Try to use

Teaching your kitten his name is easy. Simply call the name whenever you feed your pet; he will soon learn through this reward-based training to respond to his name.

the same type of tray and litter as he had in his previous home, so that the change will not be too radical – cats are creatures of habit. Bringing some of the kitten's used litter home with you and placing it in his new tray may help acclimatize him to his new facilities.

Environment and safety

Being naturally bold and curious – the world inside and outside the home is one big exciting playground to them – kittens can get into all sorts of trouble and distress if left to their own devices. See pages 22–23 and 36–39 for information on keeping your kitten or cat safe.

Going outside

After keeping your kitten indoors for a few weeks, he will have become self-confident enough to venture outside. While he is small (and only when his course of vaccinations has been completed), you should only let him out when you are around to supervise him until he gets used to his outdoor environment and is able to find his way around the garden and back into the house. This is the ideal time to introduce him to a cat flap, something self-confident kittens quickly learn to use.

Dispose of used litter, well wrapped up in newspaper or biodegradable bags, with your own household rubbish, not down the toilet, as it could cause a blockage.

Kittens are at risk from adult cats and dogs in the area, as well as other hazards, including traffic. Being cute in appearance, kittens are also much more likely to be picked up and taken home by well-meaning people who may think he has been abandoned. This is why it is so important that young cats are supervised when outside until they become 'streetwise'.

Vaccinations

For a multitude of reasons, most people are in favour of vaccinating cats, while others are against it (the frequency of booster jabs being a particular bone of contention). On balance – particularly from the veterinary point of view and in the absence of scientific evidence to prove otherwise – vaccinations are to be recommended against the nasty, often lethal diseases that cats can fall victim to. Some insurance companies insist that cats are vaccinated before they will issue policies; if vaccinations are not kept up to date, the insurers may not pay out in the event of a claim, so check the policy terms before signing up. See page 89 for further information regarding vaccinations.

Visiting the vet

Take your kitten for regular check-ups, so the vet can monitor his development and catch any potential problems early, and also so that your kitten becomes accustomed to going to the clinic and is therefore not frightened by the experience. Many vets like to see their patients just for a look-over and a little interaction, so that the animal does not view them just as someone who does only unpleasant things to him.

Veterinary health checks

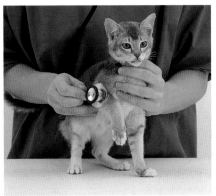

GENERAL CONDITION

Checking your kitten's body condition will tell your vet how good his physical state is.

BASIC TESTS

A full veterinary examination will involve a number of basic tests, including a heart function evaluation using a stethoscope to listen to the heartbeat.

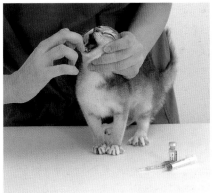

TEMPERATURE

An initial check-up is likely to include a rectal temperature reading. For ease of use and minimum discomfort for both parties, an aural thermometer is available for owners to check their pet's temperature.

TEETH

Your kitten will lose his milk teeth at the age of about five months; your vet will be able to tell if teething is occurring without problems, and, if not, will advise on treatment accordingly.

Worming

Internal parasites can cause all sorts of problems, even death, so it pays to consult your vet regarding a worming programme for your kitten. A typical regime is to deworm kittens aged four to sixteen weeks every two weeks with an appropriate roundworm product. When the kitten is six months old, it will require deworming every two to six months, depending on its lifestyle, for roundworms and tapeworms. Consult your vet for advice. (See pages 88–89 for more information.)

Flea control

If your kitten enjoys an outdoor lifestyle, or comes into contact with other cats or dogs that do, then he will almost certainly require defleaing on a regular basis. Fleas can cause all manner of unpleasant ailments, including anaemia and flea allergic dermatitis, and can be a problem all year round if not kept under control. Your vet is the best person to ask regarding a suitable flea control product for your kitten. (See pages 88–89 for more information on fleas and how to control them.)

Trimming claws

Unlike outdoor cats, who are able to keep their claws worn to a reasonable length naturally, cats that are kept indoors may need a bit of help to ensure their claws remain in good condition and do not get too long. It is easier to get kittens used to having their claws trimmed than it is to start the procedure with older cats. Ideally, claw-clipping, if necessary, should be carried out by an expert. If you do opt to do it yourself, however, ask a vet, an expert breeder or a professional cat groomer to show you how to do it – this is the best way of learning how to trim claws humanely to the correct length. They can also advise you on the correct type of clippers to purchase.

Guillotine-style claw-clippers designed for animal use are the best instrument for trimming claws.

Trimming the ends of the claws does not hurt the cat, as long as the nail bed or quick (the thin vein that runs down the nail, and which you can usually see) is not nicked; if it is, great pain will ensue – as well as profuse bleeding. If you catch the quick, the cat is unlikely ever to put up with having his claws clipped again.

Providing your kitten with a good-quality wooden scratching post (complete with bark if you can find one – perhaps even a tree branch from the garden) will help avoid the need to trim claws.

In some countries (but not in the UK where it is considered inhumane) it is legal for veterinary surgeons to completely declaw cats, although some vets will not carry out this procedure. Some owners prefer this to be done so that the cat cannot scratch them or their furniture.

Grooming

Grooming is an integral part of cat ownership. As well as helping to keep your pet's coat in good condition, carefully and gently grooming him also helps you both to bond. Depending on the coat type of your cat, you will need the right tools for the job.

Why groom?

Cats spend much of their waking time grooming, and most are able to do a good job of keeping themselves clean without much help from us. However, longhaired, infirm, arthritic and injured cats do require their owners to groom them to keep their coats in tip-top order and so help them remain mentally and physically healthy.

Long, thick hair – especially the fluffy, soft variety found in Persians – will become tangled, and then form dense mats, if it is not brushed on a regular basis. Should matting occur, grooming the coat would be far too uncomfortable for the cat, so the

FURBALLS

A furball (or hairball) is an accumulation of hair in the cat's stomach that occurs as a direct result of him grooming himself. A solid mass of hair forms which rubs against the lining of the stomach; this irritation prompts the cat to vomit the furball. If the furball lodges further down the digestive tract, it may cause a blockage; if this occurs, the cat may show signs of a decreased appetite, constipation and general lethargy. Seek veterinary attention if you suspect a furball blockage. Grooming your cat regularly will help prevent problems of this nature.

All cats produce furballs (or hairballs), but longhaired types tend to suffer more due to the quantity of hair they ingest while grooming themselves. Cats will often eat grass, which acts as an emetic, to help them vomit furballs.

Grooming guide for long coats

1 Do the back first: brush in the direction the hair is lying, working backwards from head to tail. Grooming powder can be used on especially soft coats that are prone to matting, as this will help separate the hairs, soak up excess natural coat oils and thus aid easier combing and brushing. Sprinkle the powder on and work it into the coat with your fingertips then brush and comb it all out.

2 Comb out loose hair, without pulling on any knots, as this will be painful for the cat. Gently tease these out by holding the hair near the skin with one hand while the other combs. Don't tug at a knot.

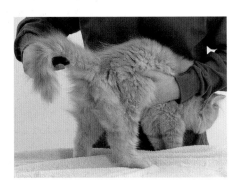

4 Use a soft brush on the tail, too, as this is very sensitive.

5 Wipe around the eyes and nose with cotton wool moistened with lukewarm water (squeezing the excess out first). Use a fresh piece for each eye and for the nose. Then very gently wipe under the tail with another piece of cotton wool. Use dry cotton wool to dry the areas wiped.

3 *With a soft bristle brush, gently brush the tummy.*

6 *A toothbrush is ideal for grooming the facial area.*
Finish off grooming by stroking the cat all over with the
grooming pad to leave a smooth, silky and shiny finish to
the coat. If the claws need trimming, do this last (see
page 62).

only alternative is to cut out the matted parts or, in very bad cases, have the coat clipped by a vet. Longhairs can also suffer from litter clumping between their toes, so always check for this when grooming, and gently tease (or carefully cut) out any mats.

Regular grooming also reduces the amount of shed hair in the house – which is especially troublesome for owners who suffer allergies.

When to groom

Grooming once a week for shorthaired cats should be sufficient, whereas longhairs ideally need daily attention. The more often you do it, the easier and quicker it is to keep the coat tangle-free, glossy and looking good. You need to pick your moment when to groom – waking the cat up to do it is not a good idea, and neither is grooming when he is fractious or unsettled for some reason. If your cat becomes fidgety and stressed by grooming, because he was not accustomed to it from an early age, then do it little and often to gradually get him used to the procedure and the invasive attention.

Never force the cat to be groomed; wait until he is in an amenable mood before trying again. Offering tiny morsels of his favourite food can help settle him and take his mind off what you are doing, as well as help him to associate grooming with something rewarding and pleasurable.

Having someone help by holding the cat can sometimes prove useful – they can talk to him and offer treats to distract him while you concentrate on the grooming.

Grooming short coats

Simply using your hand to groom will suffice for many shorthairs; this will loosen and stroke off dead hairs and tone muscles, while also being a pleasurable and soothing experience for both you and your cat.

Alternatively, use a moderately stiff

brush to brush lightly but thoroughly from head to tail to remove any loose hair. Pay particular attention to the throat, armpits and inner thighs. Next, use a fine-toothed comb all over from head to tail to remove parasites, grit, scurf and loose hairs. Then use cotton wool moistened with lukewarm water to wipe around the eyes, nose and under the tail – use a clean piece for each area. Finally, wipe over with the grooming pad to leave the coat soft and shiny.

Bathing

Cats do not usually need bathing (in fact, most hate being wet at all), unless:
• you are preparing him for a show.
• the coat has become very soiled or contaminated with chemicals or oil.
• the cat needs shampooing with a fungicidal or insecticidal wash for

When bathing your cat, take care not to get water or soap in his ears as all cats find this very distressing.

veterinary reasons (in which case you should wear protective plastic gloves). Always use a specially formulated cat shampoo and coat conditioner – never products intended for use on human hair, as these may prove harmful if absorbed through the cat's skin or accidentally ingested. You will probably need an assistant while bathing your pet, even if he has been accustomed to the procedure since kittenhood. It is easiest to bathe the cat in the kitchen sink.
• Quarter-fill the sink with lukewarm water (comfortable to the elbow-touch test) and place the cat in it.
• Ladle water over the body, until the fur is

saturated.
- Use your hands carefully to wet the cat's face.
- Massage in the shampoo, but do not get any on the face or near the eyes.
- Refill the sink with clean lukewarm water (or use a spray attachment) and rinse all the shampoo out of the coat. You will probably have to replace the water several times to ensure no soap traces remain.
- If using a separate conditioner, massage this into the coat; leave for the recommended time, then repeat the rinsing process.
- Gently dry the cat as much as you can with a thick, warm, soft towel.
- Place the cat in a warm room to dry thoroughly, and so that he does not get cold.
- Once dry, groom the coat into place.

Brushing teeth

Regularly cleaning your cat's teeth will help prevent tooth decay, gum diseases such as gingivitis, and bad breath. Toothbrushes specifically designed for kittens and cats are available from pet stores or veterinary surgeries, but a soft human toothbrush with a small head will suffice. You must not use human toothpaste – cats hate the taste and the froth it creates and they won't spit it out easily. You should also ensure that you take your cat to the vet for regular check-ups, when his teeth will be examined.

Start brushing your cat's teeth when he is a kitten, so he gets used to the treatment. Begin by simply dipping the brush in warm water, and placing it inside your kitten's cheek for a few seconds while gently holding his mouth closed. Reassure him with soothing words, and repeat with the other cheek. Do this every day, gradually extending the period the brush is held in your kitten's mouth, until he is no longer concerned about it. At this stage, begin to

Brushing your cat's teeth with a child's soft toothbrush (or one designed for cats) and special toothpaste formulated for felines (never use one intended for humans) helps to prevent tartar build-up on teeth.

move the brush in a small circle, starting with the back teeth, as these are less sensitive than the front teeth. In a few weeks you should be able to brush both the front and back teeth without causing the kitten any concern. At this stage you can introduce a small amount of feline toothpaste. Rubber finger stalls may also be used instead of a toothbrush.

Cats and travel

There are going to be occasions when you will need to be away from home –
for holidays, visiting friends and family, going into hospital, business trips –
and you will have to make arrangements for your cat to be looked after. There
are several options to choose from.

Thinking ahead

Whichever option you choose, make the
arrangements well in advance because:
- you will need to ensure your pet's
vaccinations are up to date.
- you may need to get a pet passport if you
are taking your cat abroad.
- good catteries get booked up quickly for
peak times, as do petsitters, and you need
to check them out first.
- you need to be sure that caring for your
cat is convenient for friends, family or
neighbours while you are away.
- if you are intending to take the cat with
you, you need to check whether your
accomodation is suitable for cats.
- you need to get your pet used to
travelling.

*Taking the cat's bed,
bedding and favourite toys
with him to a cattery will
help him settle and feel
more at home.*

Having a reliable person to come in at least twice a day to feed and water, clean out litter trays and provide affection can be an ideal solution for those cats who do not settle in catteries.

Boarding catteries

Seek recommendations for local boarding catteries from vets and cat-owning friends, neighbours and relatives. Visit the establishment(s) first to check them out for yourself. Your cat will need to be vaccinated against relevant diseases before entering a cattery, so ensure his injections are up to date well in advance. Take the vaccination certificate with you when you take your pet to the cattery, as they will want to check that it is in order.

The best catteries are purpose-built, with each cat having his own small cabin and outdoor run. The cabin should be clean, dry and warm, with room for a bed, food and water bowls, and the cat's belongings; the adjoining run should be secure with room for the litter tray, exercise, a 'sunning/lookout' shelf and a scratching post. Indoor catteries are not ideal as there is greater risk of infections spreading between cats because of the inadequate airflow.

Petsitters

A good option, particularly if you have a number of pets, is to arrange for a petsitter to stay in your house while you are away for any length of time. Although this can be quite expensive, it does give you peace of mind knowing that both your pet and your

Cats should always be transported in a secure carrier. The more used they are to travelling, the less disturbing they will find it.

house will be well looked after. Be sure to use a reputable agency – ideally one recommended by word of mouth – which chooses its staff carefully and offers insurance in case of any mishaps.

Petsitters are trained to look after all sorts of animals, with some specializing in and preferring particular species, so ask for someone who is cat-orientated. You can find petsitters advertised in cat magazines and on the internet.

Taking the cat with you

If you want to take your cat away with you on a regular basis within your own country, then you need to get him used to travelling, whether by car or public transport. Train him to accept this from an early age, by taking him out for short journeys. Check with public-transport companies regarding pet travel, as some have specific rules and regulations about this.

To help him feel secure, put his blanket and favourite toy(s) in the carrier. Ensure the car is not too warm and that there is plenty of ventilation, otherwise the cat may become heat-distressed. Never let him out

of the carrier, however, except in an emergency. Taking a fold-up pen with you can be a good idea, so that the cat is secure in your hotel room when you are not there.

Taking a cat abroad

Recent changes in legislation now allow for pet travel without the need for quarantine in many countries. Find out what the regulations are in your country, as the rules regarding pet travel do vary, and are constantly being updated and reviewed. To do so, contact the relevant government department (in the UK, it is the Department for the Environment, Food and Rural Affairs). The Pet Travel Scheme (PETS) now applies to pet cats and dogs that are resident in a PETS-qualifying country. Before you attempt to take your cat out of the country in which you are resident, and bring him back in again, you must find out:
• what restrictions apply.
• what you need to do to comply with rules regarding pet identification, vaccination and parasite treatment.
• how far in advance you need to do the above procedures.

AT-A-GLANCE HOLIDAY OPTIONS

CARE OPTIONS	PROS	CONS
Cattery	• Least hassle to arrange. • Safety and security. • You know your cat will be looked after properly. • Should your cat become ill or injured, he will receive appropriate and immediate treatment.	• Expensive. • Cat must be vaccinated. • Disease-carrying and sick cats will not be admitted. • Risk of contracting disease. • Cat may pine.
Visiting care at home	• No cost. • Cat can remain in familiar surroundings. • No need for vaccinations if you are against them.	• Cat will not be supervised all the time. • An only cat may get lonely. • Can you rely on the carer to see to your cat at least once a day and care for him properly? • If the cat becomes ill or injured, he may not get adequate immediate treatment.
Staying with carer	• No cost. • Cat will possibly have company all the time. • No need to vaccinate.	• Cat may escape and get lost. • Cat may not settle well in unfamiliar territory and become depressed or develop behavioural problems.
Petsitter	• Cat will have experienced company and care all the time. • No need to vaccinate. • Your house will also be looked after.	• Expensive. • You may not want a stranger in your home.
Taking your cat with you	• You know your cat is receiving your proper and appropriate attention. • Your cat will have company all of the time.	• It can be difficult to find cat-friendly accommodation. • Organizing PETS eligibility when going abroad (see page 70) can prove expensive and complicated. • Your cat may escape and get lost. • Your cat may not enjoy travelling. • Your cat may not settle well. • Your cat may contract a disease.

The feline body

The feline body is a remarkable feat of natural engineering that has evolved into an animal possessing great beauty, grace and athletic prowess. To keep your cat in peak condition, it helps to know how your pet's body is constructed; how it works; how to recognize when something is wrong; what to do when your cat is ill or injured.

Bones in the feline body

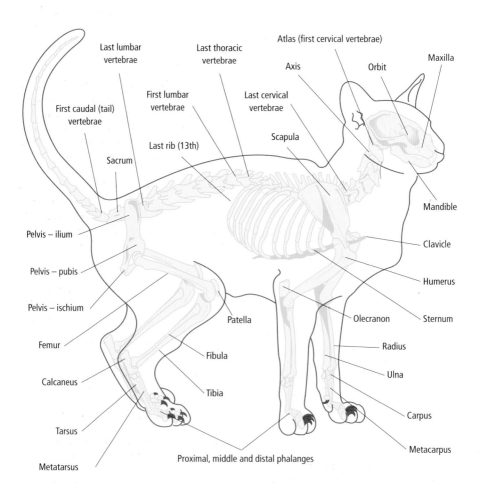

Last lumbar vertebrae

Last thoracic vertebrae

Atlas (first cervical vertebrae)

Axis

Orbit

Maxilla

First lumbar vertebrae

Last cervical vertebrae

First caudal (tail) vertebrae

Scapula

Last rib (13th)

Sacrum

Mandible

Pelvis – ilium

Clavicle

Pelvis – pubis

Humerus

Pelvis – ischium

Patella

Olecranon

Sternum

Femur

Fibula

Radius

Calcaneus

Ulna

Tibia

Tarsus

Carpus

Metatarsus

Proximal, middle and distal phalanges

Metacarpus

Bones

A cat's body may be much smaller than a human's, but it contains more bones – some 230 to a human's 206. The skeleton of a cat is made up of a semi-rigid framework that supports other, softer structures.

The bones of the spine, limbs, shoulders and pelvis (working together with muscles and tendons), comprise a system of efficient levers to aid movement, while the skull, ribcage and pelvis protect the major organs they contain.

There are four distinct types of bone – long, short, irregular and flat bones – and each type has a particular function. They are joined together to make up the skeleton via tendons and ligaments.

Long bones

These are cylindrical and have hollow shafts that contain the vital bone marrow in which blood cells are manufactured. They form the cat's limbs. Feline long bones are the humerus, radius, femur (thigh bone), tibia and fibula.

Short bones

These consist of a spongy core surrounded by compact bones. They are the bones in the feet and the patella (kneecap – where the femur articulates with the tibia).

Irregular bones

So called because of their irregular shapes, these bones are similar in structure to short bones. A long string of irregular bones make up the spine (vertebral column) and tail. The irregular projections of the bones in the spinal column serve as attachment points for the various muscles of the cat's back.

Flat bones

These are made of two layers of compact bone with a spongy layer sandwiched between them, and comprise the skull, pelvis and shoulder blades (scapulae). Flattened and elongated bones make up the cat's 13 pairs of ribs; these bones are not hollow but contain a substantial amount of marrow, which produces blood cells.

Muscular system

Overlying the skeletal framework is a complex network of muscles that gives the cat his powerful and graceful movement, and is also responsible for his sinuous shape. There are three types of muscle in the feline body: cardiac, smooth (involuntary) and striped (voluntary).

Cardiac muscle

This specialized muscle forms the heart, and possesses unique powers of rhythmic contraction to pump blood around the body through a network of arteries and veins. Similar to the human heart, it has four chambers and a double pump.

Smooth (unstriated) muscles

Also called involuntary muscles, these carry out muscular functions not under the cat's control, and include the muscles of the intestines and walls of blood vessels.

Striped (striated) muscles

These are muscle tissues in which the contractile fibres are arranged in parallel bundles (hence the term 'striped') and are

LIGAMENTS AND TENDONS

Ligaments are short bands of tough, fibrous connective tissue that connect bones or cartilage, or hold together a joint. They are also membranous folds that support organs and keep them in position.

Tendons are flexible but inelastic cords of strong fibrous tissue attaching muscles to bone.

attached to the limbs and other parts of the anatomy which are under the voluntary control of the cat – such as movement. They are also known as voluntary muscles.

Voluntary muscles are usually attached to bones that form a joint. **Extensor muscles** extend and straighten a limb, while **flexor muscles** flex and bend the joint. Muscles that move a limb away from the body are called **abductors**, and **adductors** move them back in again. There are more than 500 voluntary muscles within a cat's body, enabling him to be fluid and controlled in his movements.

Respiratory system

Respiration provides the cat's body with the oxygen that is vital for life. During respiration, the cat draws in air through his nasal passages via his nose and mouth. This air passes through the throat (pharynx) and down the windpipe (trachea), through the bronchi and into the lungs, where a gaseous exchange takes place – carbon dioxide from the blood filters into the air sacs as oxygen passes from the air to replenish the blood. The used air is then exhaled. Breathing is automatic: chest muscles contract and relax, acting like a pump on the ribs and diaphragm, driving air in and out of the lungs. The breathing rate varies in each individual and depends upon:
• age
• exercise
• emotion
• environmental temperature
The normal respiration rate of a healthy, resting, adult cat is 20–30 breaths per minute.

Circulatory system

Every body cell needs a supply of nourishment, and this is achieved via the blood, which delivers it and also removes waste products from the body. Blood is made up of red blood cells and white blood corpuscles that are contained in a fluid called plasma. Plasma contains platelets which contain a blood-clotting agent for use in the event of cuts and wounds.

Red blood cells transport oxygen, while white blood corpuscles collect and transport impurities and bacteria that have invaded the red cells.

Incredible journey

Blood is continually pumped around the body via the four-chambered heart, its journey beginning in the left auricle (upper chamber). Enriched with oxygen from the lungs, the blood from the left auricle travels into the left ventricle (lower chamber), and on into a great artery – the aorta – to run its

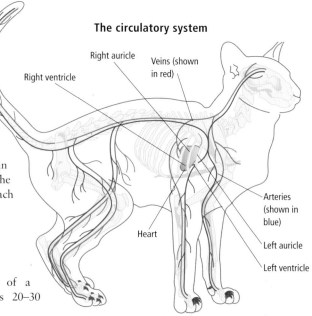

The circulatory system

Right auricle

Veins (shown in red)

Right ventricle

Arteries (shown in blue)

Heart

Left auricle

Left ventricle

course quickly through all the arteries and arterioles and into a fine network of capillaries throughout the body, distributing its store of oxygen and nutrients as it goes. As it releases these, the blood collects waste matter (bacteria, dead blood cells and carbon dioxide).

Leaving the capillaries, the blood enters tiny veins (venules) where, laden with waste products, it begins to slow down before passing into the great veins that transport it back to the lungs to dump its rubbish and be replenished with oxygen and nutrients. It then enters the heart to repeat its journey.

Why cats are usually sleepy after meals

Extra nutrient-rich blood with its nutrients is required by different parts of the body at different times. After a heavy meal, for example, the cat's abdomen draws in extra blood to aid digestion, at the expense of the supply to the brain and other parts of the body. Hence the need of the cat (and indeed other animals) to rest or sleep after eating – the brain is less active and energy is being utilized in digestion rather than in other activities.

Pulse

Blood passing through the aorta causes its walls to expand, and a pressure wave (pulse) passes down the arteries. In a healthy adult cat at rest, depending on the cat's emotional state and the environmental temperature at the time, the pulse rate is 160–240 beats per minute

Digestive system

The cat's digestive system is adapted for a meat-eating hunter that may not always be successful in catching a meal, so may occasionally gorge at a large kill. His mouth construction means that a cat tears or bites at his food, then swallows it quickly, giving the salivary juices virtually no time for the preliminary breakdown of starches into blood sugars. Any starches present in the cat's diet are, therefore, of little nutritional value.

Feline gastric juices are more powerful than those of a human; they are, in fact, strong enough to soften bone. Cats can swallow large chunks of prey creatures (rodents and birds) and any parts such as feathers, hair and bones that are not quickly broken down in the stomach may be regurgitated.

In the stomach, protein is broken down into simple amino acids (basic constituents of proteins). These are then combined to form the building blocks necessary for replacement of cells throughout the cat's

The major organs

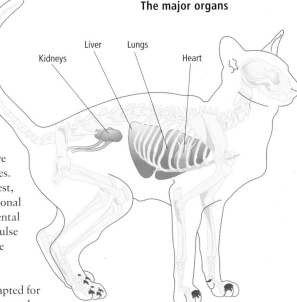

Liver Lungs Heart

Kidneys

body. From the stomach, partly digested food passes through a valve called the pylorus to the small intestine. Further digestion changes take place, aided by secretions from the pancreas and liver. Fats are broken down and extracted, sugars are changed structurally (ready for storage) and minerals are absorbed.

From the small intestine, the now-fluid food contents pass into the large intestine, where they are acted upon by the specialized bacteria present there. Excess water is drawn off and utilized where appropriate, and the waste passes through the colon to be voided as faeces (solids) or as urine (liquid).

Teeth

Feline teeth are designed to stab, slice and tear at raw, tough food rather than chew it, and these actions help keep the teeth in good condition. Kittens shed their baby (milk) teeth as their permanent ones come through at around six months. When kittens are born, the teeth are just visible inside the gums, and soon erupt. At six weeks old, a kitten's teeth are strong and needle-sharp so, for obvious reasons, a mother cat will become reluctant to feed her babies, and a natural weaning process takes place, with the youngsters, ideally, having strips of raw meat to chew on.

Occasionally, 'double dentition' occurs, when a kitten does not shed his milk teeth. It may be necessary in such cases for a vet to remove the problem milk teeth so that they do not interfere with secondary tooth growth and action, which could ultimately lead to digestive and other health problems.

Paws and claws

A cat's fore paws are made up of sets of three small bones, each of which forms a digit corresponding to the finger of the human hand. The tiny bones at the end of

The skull and teeth

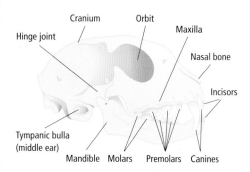

each digit are highly specialized and articulate so that the claws may be extended or contracted at will. The cat has no thumb, but a corresponding digit that comprises two bones that form the dew claw. In the hind feet the bones are longer and the first toe is absent altogether.

Claws are made up of keratin (the same material which forms hair), and grow continuously from the base, like human fingernails. There are five claws on the fore paws and four on each hind paw – the fifth claw acts rather like our thumb, helping the cat to grip when climbing or holding prey.

Cats with extra digits (polydactyls)

Occasionally, a cat has more digits than is normal on either or both of the fore and hind paws. This anomaly sometimes occurs in cross-breeds, and is nothing to be concerned about (being no more than a gene mutation) because it does not usually affect a cat's health or movement. If, however, this condition occurs in pedigree cats, it has more serious implications for the breeder, though not for the cat. The cat will not conform to breed standards, and so will have little value. Pedigree cats who are afflicted should therefore not be bred from, so as not to perpetuate the condition.

Skin and fur

Feline skin is made up of two layers of tissue: the **dermis** (inner layer), and the **epidermis** (outer layer), which is constantly being replaced as it dies and sloughs away into tiny flakes of dandruff (dead skin). There are sweat glands on the skin, but these seem to exist mainly for excreting impurities from the body rather than for controlling body temperature. True sweat glands are to be found in the foot pads.

Sebaceous glands open into the hair follicles and produce a semi-liquid, oily substance, called sebum, to coat each new hair as it grows. Scent glands can be found on the forehead just above the eyes (temporal glands), by the lips (perioral glands) and near the root of the tail.

Hair is derived from the outer layer of skin, and acts as insulatory cover. It is modified in certain areas to provide eyelashes, eyebrows and whiskers. There are three main types of hair.

• **Down hairs** or undercoat hairs are the shortest, thinnest and softest hairs; they lie close to the body and conserve body heat.

• **Awn hairs** form the middle coat and are slightly more bristly, with a swelling towards the tip before it tapers off. They are partly for insulation and partly for protection.

• **Guard hairs** are the thickest, longest and straightest; they form the top coat, which protects the fur below from the elements.

The ratio of down, awn and guard hairs varies greatly between the domestic breeds; in the wildcat, there are approximately 1,000 down hairs to 300 awn hairs and 20 guard hairs. Muscles attached to the large follicles enable the hairs to become erect and stand out at right angles to the skin; this occurs, for example, when the cat is ill and has an abnormal temperature.

All hairs, especially the guard hairs, are sensitive to the touch, but even more

The skin and fur

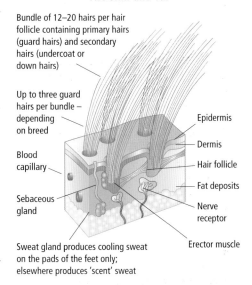

Bundle of 12–20 hairs per hair follicle containing primary hairs (guard hairs) and secondary hairs (undercoat or down hairs)

Up to three guard hairs per bundle – depending on breed

Blood capillary

Sebaceous gland

Epidermis

Dermis

Hair follicle

Fat deposits

Nerve receptor

Erector muscle

Sweat gland produces cooling sweat on the pads of the feet only; elsewhere produces 'scent' sweat

sensitive are the **vibrissae** (whiskers, eyebrows and similar hairs on the cheeks, chin and behind the forelegs), which are bigger and thicker. Whiskers are deeply embedded in the upper lip and are surrounded by a mass of tiny nerve endings which transmit information about any contact they make and changes in air pressure around them. The vibrissae also act as guides when it is too dark to see, enabling the cat to move without banging into objects.

Cats shed dead hair constantly (especially those that live in centrally heated environments), but those that spend a good deal of time outdoors will grow a thicker winter coat, and then shed this as the temperature warms up again in spring; it is not unusual for their coats to appear quite patchy during this time.

Feline senses

The nervous and sensory systems of the cat are essential to his health and well-being. Perceptions and reactions to his environment are dependent on his senses; movement is controlled via the central nervous system (brain and spinal cord); and the endocrine system (hormone-producing glands) controls his behaviour patterns.

The central nervous system

This controls and co-ordinates the cat's everyday activities. Information received by the sensory organs is constantly monitored by the system and dealt with according to its importance. It is acted upon immediately, discarded or stored away for future use, as appropriate. The brain has three clearly defined regions: the fore-brain, the mid-brain and the hind-brain.

Fore-brain

This area is concerned with the sense of smell via the olfactory lobe, memory and intelligence. It also contains the thalamus (which responds to impulses travelling from the spinal cord) and the hypothalamus (which controls the internal regulatory processes).

Mid-brain

This contains the optic lobes and deals with signals stimulated by light; therefore it is responsible for sight.

Hind-brain (core)

Here, the cerebellum controls balance and the enlarged end of the spinal cord forms

The brain and its functions

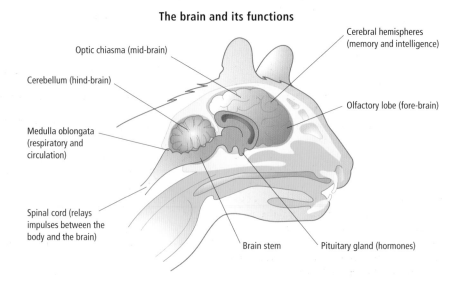

Optic chiasma (mid-brain)

Cerebellum (hind-brain)

Medulla oblongata (respiratory and circulation)

Spinal cord (relays impulses between the body and the brain)

Cerebral hemispheres (memory and intelligence)

Olfactory lobe (fore-brain)

Brain stem

Pituitary gland (hormones)

the medulla, controlling the respiratory and circulatory systems. The pituitary gland (which produces hormones) is situated in this region, as is the limbic system that controls digestion of foods. Unsurprisingly, this part of the brain is vital for the survival of the cat.

Sight

Cats need only one-sixth of the light humans need in order to distinguish the same detail of shape and movement. The eyes face forwards, allowing fields of vision to overlap and giving stereoscopic vision that is slightly wider than ours. This enables the cat to be accurate in judging distances for jumping, or springing and pouncing when hunting for food.

Being comparatively large, and set in deep skull sockets, feline eyes do not move freely, so the cat turns his head to bring objects into sharp focus. Cats are not colour-blind, but see the world in more subtle shades of colour than we do. Their eyes are protected from strong light by the iris contracting to form a slit-like pupil, limiting the amount of light reaching the delicate mechanisms at the back of the eye; when the iris contracts, the sharpness of vision is enhanced. In addition to the upper and lower eyelids, there is a third eyelid, which is called the nictitating membrane or haw. This is a thin sheet of pale tissue tucked away in the corner of the eye. Its function is to remove dust and dirt from the cornea by moving across the surface of the eyeball during any inward movement, and also to keep it moist and lubricated.

The central nervous system

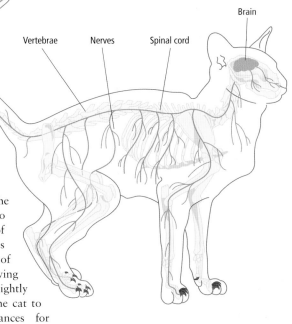

Vertebrae   Nerves   Spinal cord   Brain

The eye

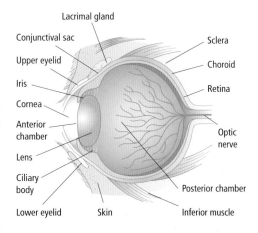

Lacrimal gland
Conjunctival sac
Upper eyelid
Iris
Cornea
Anterior chamber
Lens
Ciliary body
Lower eyelid
Skin
Sclera
Choroid
Retina
Optic nerve
Posterior chamber
Inferior muscle

Smell

The feline sense of smell is about 30 times more developed than that of humans, and is essential to cats in relation to their sex life and hunting for food and water. A thick spongy membrane (olfactory mucosa) in the nose, with over twice the surface area of that of humans, contains 200 million scent-sensitive cells. When minute particles of odorous substances in the atmosphere are drawn in during normal breathing, they stimulate highly sensitive nerve endings of fine hairs within the nasal cavities.

In the roof of the mouth there is a special organ lined with receptor cells. Known as the vomeronasal or Jacobson's organ, it is a tube, 1.2 cm (½ in) long, with its opening just behind the front teeth. Interesting odours are sucked into the mouth and directed to the Jacobson's organ to be investigated in more detail. The facial expression cats execute to do this (open mouth, lips drawn back and wrinkled nose) is called the Flehmen reaction.

Hearing

Feline hearing is exceptionally well developed, and cats can hear noises that are quite inaudible to the human ear. They can hear ultrasonic sounds that precede an activity, which is why they often react before we are even aware that anything is happening. The ear is made up of three sections: the outer, middle and inner ear.

The outer ear

The ear flap (pinna) acts as a funnel to direct sound waves down to the eardrum which is tautly stretched across the ear canal, separating it from the middle ear. The eardrum vibrates in response to sound waves.

The middle ear

In here, three small bones – the hammer (malleus), anvil (incus) and stirrup (stapes) – transmit the sound relayed from the eardrum to the cochlea, which is contained within the inner ear.

When familiar cats meet, sniffing each other confirms visual recognition and gathers information about how the other cat is, where he has been and what he has been doing.

The ear

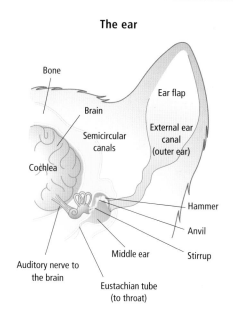

Bone
Brain
Ear flap
Semicircular canals
External ear canal (outer ear)
Cochlea
Hammer
Anvil
Auditory nerve to the brain
Middle ear
Stirrup
Eustachian tube (to throat)

Large ear flaps help a cat to focus sound and judge where it is coming from, thereby enabling him to pinpoint the position of prey even if he cannot see it.

The inner ear

The cochlea is a spiral cavity, containing the organ of Corti that converts the sound vibrations transmitted from the middle ear into nerve impulses. These are then passed along the acoustic nerve to the auditory cortex of the brain, where they are decoded and recognized by comparison with sounds stored in the memory bank.

Taste

It seems that the cat's tongue can differentiate between food items that taste salty, sour or bitter. Most cats appear to like salty things, but are virtually unable to taste sweet flavours. Taste alone does not seem to be important to most cats, but this is how tiny kittens, on first leaving the nest, test most new surfaces and objects – by licking them carefully and methodically, and with great concentration. Just how the information received in this way is analysed and stored is not known, and it occurs only during the most sensitive period of learning.

Touch

Cats use their noses, paws and whiskers for examining objects by touch, after having first checked them out by smell. They rarely burn themselves with hot foods or liquids, as they use their noses as thermometers to test for temperature. Their whiskers are used to judge space on either side of them and how close they are to objects in the dark. Affectionate cats will often pat at their owner's faces or bodies to attract attention. Hunting cats touch prey with a paw to see if it is dead or alive. Mother cats often touch their kittens with their faces and paws. Cats also use their faces, whiskers and paws to touch each other.

Routine health care

Knowing your cat, and his usual behaviour, will help you recognize when something is not quite right with him. If ailments are spotted quickly, then early treatment often helps to prevent more serious problems occurring; this usually results in less suffering for your pet and smaller veterinary bills for you. Monitoring your cat's mood and habits, and carrying out simple health checks on a regular basis, will enable you to assess his state of health.

Regular home checks

Keep an eye on all the following aspects of your cat's health, condition and demeanour.

General condition, skin and fur

The healthy cat is alert, interested in what is going on around him, curious, and looks well in himself. The skin should be clean, supple and pliable, while the fur should be soft and glossy, not dull and lank. Check for parasites, wounds, scurf, lumps and scabs.

Appetite and thirst

Any change from normal eating and drinking patterns can indicate a digestive, urinary or mouth problem, and if this occurs it is essential to take your cat to a vet as soon as possible.

Grooming

A healthy cat constantly cleans and grooms his fur. A sick cat will neglect himself in this department and soon begin to look scruffy. Reasons for failure to wash include mouth soreness and joint stiffness (which could indicate arthritis), while female cats that stop cleaning their genital region could have a distasteful discharge.

Mouth and teeth

Cat breath should not be offensive: tooth disorders are easy to diagnose because of the resulting unpleasant smell. The mouth area and tongue should be pale pink in colour – white gums indicate anaemia, red bleeding gums are an indication of gingivitis (see page 107–108), and blue or grey gums suggest a circulatory problem. If your cat shows a reluctance or inability to

HEALTH CONCERNS AT A GLANCE

- Blood in urine or faeces.
- Breathing difficulty.
- Coughing or sneezing.
- Diarrhoea/constipation.
- Difficulty in eating.
- Difficulty in eliminating.
- Dullness or fever.
- Fur loss or failure to self-groom.
- Haws showing.
- Increased or decreased thirst.
- Lameness.
- Loss of appetite.
- Marked change in behaviour.
- Nasal discharge.
- Pallor of lips and gums.
- Scratching or licking.
- Signs of acute pain.
- Stiff or unsteady gait.
- Swollen abdomen.
- Ulceration of mouth.
- Vomiting.
- Weight loss or increase.

If your vet knows your cat almost as well as you do, this familiarity often makes treating him more efficient and successful.

eat, seek veterinary advice, as this could be due to a mouth abscess, a broken tooth or some other more serious ailment.

Eyes, ears and nose

The eyes should be clear, bright and free from discharge. Some breeds of cat with 'typey' facial features often suffer from eye discharge; this occurs as a result of the skull structure being deformed, meaning that tears cannot drain away as they would normally. Tearstains can be removed with cotton wool dipped in clean, boiled and cooled water. Any clouding of the surface of the eye requires veterinary attention. The pupils should be of the same size and the third eyelid (haw) retracted.

The inner ear surface should be clean, smooth and odour-free, and feel slightly greasy to the touch. Smelly or dirty ears need veterinary investigation, as this suggests there may be infection present.

The nose should be clean, slightly damp and free from discharge. Runny noses are often a sign of viral infection or allergy.

Weight

Cats, like humans, vary greatly in size and conformation. The average adult weight of a cat is around 4–5 kg (9–11 lb); a small cat may weigh only 2.5 kg (5 lb 8 oz) and a large one as much as 5.5 kg (12 lb). Your vet will be able to tell you what your cat's ideal weight should be, and any deviation from this should be closely monitored. Obese cats have a shorter life expectancy than those of the correct weight, as carrying excess weight puts a strain on the heart and

Administering medicine and pills

Only give medication as prescribed or advised by your vet, and administer it as directed. It helps to have someone to hold the cat while you give medicine or pills to him.

SYRINGE

Giving medicine via a syringe (your vet can supply these) is the easiest way to administer it. Insert the nozzle in the corner of the mouth and squeeze a little at a time, stroking the cat's throat to encourage him to swallow.

PILL–GIVER

Administer pills using a pill-giver (obtainable from vets), or with your fingers – although the latter can be more difficult. Tip the cat's head back as shown and insert the pill into the mouth, then gently hold the mouth shut.

AIDING SWALLOWING

To encourage the cat to swallow the pill, gently stroke his throat.

Applying topical treatments

ADMINISTERING EYE DROPS

Only use treatments prescribed by your vet and apply them as directed. When administering drops or ointment to the eye, hold the cat's head still and aim for the centre of the eye.

ADMINISTERING EAR DROPS

To apply ear drops, hold your cat's head still, squeeze in the drops, and then gently massage the base of the ear to ensure the liquid is evenly distributed on the affected internal area. Do not poke anything into the ear canal.

limbs. Weight loss can indicate internal disease, such as parasites or pancreatic problems. Seek veterinary advice.

Faeces and urine

If your cat has difficulty in defecating or urinating, he needs very urgent veterinary attention. Stools should be firm, but not hard or loose, while urine should be pale yellow in colour and free from clouding and an offensive smell. Both should be free from traces of blood.

Ease of movement

Stiffness when moving around could indicate joint problems. Limping suggests a direct pain source such as a fractured limb,

a wound, a thorn stuck in the foot pad or an infected claw bed. A general reluctance to move around, combined with crying out when picked up, or even when touched, may be due to an internal injury or ailment.

Veterinary health checks

Choose a vet who specializes in feline health, and make the effort to cultivate a good relationship with him or her. An owner who takes their cat for regular health checks and routine vaccinations, and seeks advice on parasite control and dental care, is a valued customer for whom a vet will be prepared to give more time.

Take your pet for a check-up at least once a year (combine this with the annual

vaccination booster), and every six months for old cats (aged 10 or more); this can often identify health problems before they become serious. Keeping a diary of your pet's behaviour and health, and being able to explain any changes you have noticed, including when these first occurred, is very useful in helping your vet treat your cat appropriately and swiftly.

Parasite control

Cats, especially those with access to outdoors, can suffer from a variety of external and internal parasites, including lice, fleas, fungal infections, ticks and

Ideally, cats should be 100 per cent well before vaccinations are given, to reduce the risk of an adverse reaction to them.

worms – all of which cause ill health. There is a wide variety of preparations available to buy off the shelf at pet stores and supermarkets designed to treat these parasites, but they are not as effective as those that are available on prescription from your vet. So, while the former products may be cheaper and easier to obtain, they often prove to be false economy in the long run.

DISEASES TO VACCINATE AGAINST

- Feline leukaemia virus (FeLV), see page 115.
- Cat flu (feline respiratory disease) – there are two forms of this disease:
feline herpes virus (also known as feline rhinotracheitis virus) and feline calici virus (FCV), see page 107.
- Feline infectious enteritis (FIE), also known as feline panleukopenia, see page 114.
- Chlamydial disease, see page 112.
- Rabies.
- Feline infectious peritonitis (FIP) – the vaccination is currently available only in the USA, see page 116.

Never use more than one defleaing treatment at a time, otherwise your cat may overdose. You must also treat the indoor environment where your cat lives, or reinfestation will occur immediately. Vacuum-clean carpets and wherever your cat likes to sleep regularly, and wash your pet's bedding once a week or so to destroy flea eggs.

Intestinal worms (roundworm and tapeworm) are most efficiently controlled via all-in-one treatments prescribed and administered by your vet. A typical worming regime is to treat kittens aged four to sixteen weeks for roundworms every fortnight; from six months old, treat the cat every two to six months (depending on whether he is an outdoor or an indoor cat) for both roundworm and tapeworm. Consult your vet for advice about the most appropriate worming plan and treatment for your cat.

Vaccination

Cats, like any other animals, are susceptible to certain viral diseases, some of which can prove fatal. While they will not pass these on to humans (apart from rabies), they will transfer them to other cats, either in the air or through mating or other physical contact. It is advisable to have your cat vaccinated in order to:
- help prevent your cat dying early from a feline viral disease.
- help prevent feline viral diseases reaching epidemic proportions.
- help eliminate feline viral diseases.
- enable you to book your cat into a cattery when you go on holiday.
- enable him to enter cat shows.
- enable you to travel abroad with your cat if you so wish.

When to vaccinate

Vaccinations are given via injection by a vet. Kittens can receive their first shots at about nine weeks of age, with a second dose given at 12 weeks. Full protection is not achieved until seven to ten days after the second vaccination. Thereafter, cats should receive annual or two-yearly boosters to maintain their level of immunity (depending on advice from the vet and whether tests are carried out to ascertain the level of immunity) and also to satisfy boarding cattery, passport and show-entry requirements.

Vaccination risks

There are some risks associated with vaccination, but these are generally low and severe reactions are rare. Your cat may have a small lump at the injection site, or may be quiet and off his food, for 24 hours after immunization, but should soon recover. If you are worried about your pet's behaviour or health after vaccination, contact your vet immediately for advice. On the whole, most vets recommend immunization to prevent certain life-threatening feline diseases reaching epidemic proportions, especially in urban areas where there are large numbers of cats in close proximity.

Neutering

If you are going to breed from your cat, you will have a clear idea of whether you want to raise kittens or set up a stud. If not, and your cat is to be a pet only, then he or she should be neutered.

Why neutering is a good idea

A mature, unneutered male cat needs to pass on his genes. Since defending a sizeable territory, competing with rivals and courting females requires large amounts of energy, tomcats often look thin and ragged, with numerous scars and abscesses from countless fights. Straying, too, can become a problem with both male and female cats as they seek a mate (see page 44).

As well as the risk of unwanted kittens, there is also the real risk of cats passing on diseases such as feline immunodeficiency virus (FIV) – the cat virus related to AIDS.

When to neuter

Neutering (spaying in females and castration in males) should be carried out when the cat reaches sexual maturity at around six months, or at any time afterwards. Individual vets have their own policy on spaying in-season females. This is because the reproductive organs have an increased supply of blood, so there can be greater risks in surgery. The neutering of pedigree or show cats is often delayed to allow their full physical development.

What is involved?

Because the operation is more involved with females, spaying is more expensive than castration. Some animal charities have low-

Neutering removes the great responsibility of having to find good, loving homes for kittens.

cost neutering schemes to help those owners on low income. Ask the staff at your local veterinary clinic, or contact animal charities in your area, if you qualify.

Spaying females

Under a general anaesthetic the vet will shave and clean the operation area, then make a small incision from the navel towards the hind legs, or in the flank, to remove the ovaries, fallopian tubes and uterus. They close the wound with two or three stitches, which they will remove about one week later – unless they are using soluble stitches which gradually dissolve on their own.

Castrating males

The vet anaesthetizes the cat and removes his testes and part of the spermatic cord through an incision in the scrotum; this incision is so small that it does not require stitches.

Pre- and post-operative care

The cat must go without food and water for 12 hours before the operation, but most cats are up and about within a few hours of their operation.

SPAYING AND CASTRATION

SPAYING

Before spaying: the female reproductive tract comprises the ovaries, fallopian tubes and uterus (womb).

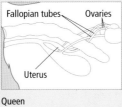

Queen

After spaying: the ovaries, fallopian tubes and uterus have been removed.

Spayed female

CASTRATION

Before castration: the male reproductive tract comprises two testicles (testes) within a skin sac (scrotum), connected to the penis via the vas deferens (spermatic cord).

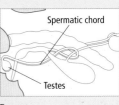

Tom cat

After castration: the testicles and part of the vas deferens have been removed.

Neutered male

When you bring the cat home from the vet's, he or she will probably still be drowsy, so put him or her in a warm, quiet place to rest – with water, a litter tray and a light meal of cooked white fish or chicken. Your vet will advise whether to keep the cat inside or can allow it out. Gently discourage the cat from nibbling or excessively licking any stitches. If you have any worries at all following neutering, contact your vet for advice. If you can't stop her from chewing the stitches ask the vet for an Elizabethan collar.

Neuter behaviour

If neutered as kittens, the behaviour of male and female cats will be similar to before the operation. Minor changes to expect include reduced terrifory size and fewer fights with other cats, a more affectionate and amenable cat who spends more time at home, and males being less inclined to spray.

Neutered cats do tend to become more inactive than unneutered ones as they age, although their life expectancy is greater. You may have to feed him less and play with him every day to encourage him to exercise.

Contraception

It is possible to administer a hormone treatment to female cats to prevent unwanted pregnancies, but there are drawbacks to prolonged birth-control treatment. It could cause fertility problems if you wish to breed from the cat later and may result in side-effects such as increased appetite, weight gain, lethargy, behavioural problems and uterine disease.

You can also use contraceptive drugs to prevent an unwanted pregnancy once mating has taken place (misalliance). This involves the vet giving an injection of hormones that override the queen's own hormones, making her body believe she is not pregnant. This causes her to come into season (oestrus) again. Some vets do not like to give this treatment, since it can have serious side-effects such as the development of pyometra (a life-threatening infection of the uterus).

Conception, pregnancy and birth

The urge to reproduce and pass genes on to the next generation is strong in unneutered felines, and a healthy female cat with access to males and a plentiful food supply can produce two or three litters of kittens a year. Species survival depends upon procreation, and pregnancy and birth are the most natural things in the world. Left to their own devices, cat courtship is a noisy affair, with several males attempting to mate with an in-season and responsive female, but usually one male is able to keep the others away and mate successfully.

Mating and conception

As the female (queen) becomes ready to mate she rolls flirtatiously on the ground to attract males – queens should be dewormed well before mating takes place. Courtship can be a prolonged affair: despite wanting to mate, the female does not immediately accept the male's approach. When she does eventually accept him, the male firmly grips the back of the female's neck to hold her steady as he mounts her and mates.

After mating, as the male withdraws, barbs on the end of his penis, which stimulate the female to ovulate, cause pain inside the female. This makes her cry out, and she then turns on him in self-defence. At this point, the male makes a hasty exit in case the female strikes out at him. His involvement in the reproduction process is now complete.

After copulation, the female rolls on the ground and then washes herself. Minutes later, she may be ready to mate again – this increases her chances of successfully becoming pregnant.

Looking after the pregnant queen

Apart from increasing her diet with food specially formulated for expectant queens to cope with the demands being made on their bodies (see pages 20–21), treat the mother as normal during pregnancy. About halfway through the pregnancy, she will become more careful about jumping and

Newborn kittens' eyes are sealed shut and begin to open at about 10 days old, although they may open as early as the middle of the first week.

Queens will move their kittens if they do not feel safe, or if the nest becomes dirty or flea-infested. The kittens go limp when she picks them up by the scruff of the neck, which does not hurt them and helps her carry them more easily.

passing through narrow openings, owing to her enlarged shape.

Take great care when picking her up and cuddling her as her pregnancy progresses – she may well not appreciate either, being uncomfortably full of kittens. If she becomes constipated, substitute one of her daily meals with oily food, such as pilchards, as this will aid the passing of motions.

Prepare a kittening nest, and place it in a quiet and undisturbed area of the house: a large sturdy cardboard box will do, with a hole cut into one side 15 cm (6 in) off the ground and wide enough for the cat to pass through easily. Line the base with newspaper for insulation and place a thick layer of paper towels on top to make a soft, absorbent and disposable mattress for the birth. Show the queen where the nest is; bear in mind, however, that she may ultimately choose her own place – which could even be on or under your bed.

With longhaired queens, clip hair surrounding the birth canal (to aid hygiene and ease of delivery) and nipples (to facilitate ease of suckling). Gently sponge her anal area twice a day if she is carrying a large litter and is unable to clean this herself. Make sure she is free of fleas and mites in the 10 days preceding the birth – consult your vet regarding suitable treatment for a pregnant cat.

Pregnancy, labour and birth

The gestation period in cats is nine weeks (approximately 63 days). Movement of the foetuses can be felt from the seventh week of pregnancy. As the birth nears, the female will begin to 'nest' and seek a private, preferably dark, safe place in which to give birth.

Females give birth and raise their young following instinctive behaviour patterns that allow them to do so unaided, although they do get better at this with practice. In a natural colony of cats, however, other related females will help out, acting as midwives and surrogate nurses while the mother takes a break. This co-operation ensures greater protection and survival of the young.

There are two stages to labour. First-stage labour involves the queen pacing around crying or growling softly. She will keep looking behind her in an agitated and puzzled manner. As second-stage labour begins, the queen goes into her nesting area or box, lies on her side and strains as uterine contractions move the kittens, one at a time, down the birth canal.

Labour and birth normally proceed easily. Once second-stage labour begins, a whole litter may be born in an hour or so, or they may be spread over 24 hours with long rests between kittens.

After delivering a kitten, the queen cleans away the birth membrane covering it, thus allowing and stimulating him to breathe. She passes the placenta, joined to the kitten by the umbilical cord, and eats it, severing the cord a short way from the kitten's body. Once all the kittens are born, the queen cleans herself, then settles down to suckle her babies, curling herself around them, and rests for about 12 hours.

Birth problems

Occasionally things do go wrong. If the queen has been straining hard for 30 minutes without results, call a vet immediately to help her give birth. Sometimes, for various reasons, kittens do not survive. If the bereaved mother cat appears distressed, contact your vet for advice: the queen may require medication to suppress her milk and help prevent

ORPHANED KITTENS

In the rare instances when unweaned kittens are abandoned or orphaned, it is necessary to hand-rear them. This is a hugely time-consuming and tiring business, although it is usually ultimately rewarding if the helpless babies grow into healthy and independent young cats. If the kittens are left without a mother for whatever reason, consult your vet immediately – he or she may know of a potential feline foster mother, or be able to put you in touch with an experienced breeder for tips, or they may offer advice themselves on how to hand-rear the kittens.

potential mastitis, or her loss may have a happy ending if the vet knows of orphaned kittens needing a foster mum. Other problems that can arise during pregnancy or following birth include:
• **miscarriage**, due to illness or because the foetuses are not healthy.
• **uterine infection** after birth, indicated by fever, vomiting, lack of appetite, dark coloured vaginal discharge.
• **prolapsed uterus**, indicated by a swollen red mass appearing out of the vulva.

It is important to consult your vet immediately if any of these problems occur.

A large cat pen, complete with litter tray, in which to put the
kittens for brief periods when weaning begins, will provide the
mother cat with periods of much-needed rest. It will also
encourage the kittens to use the tray.

The mother encourages her kittens to play from an early age.
Through play, the kittens practise social, fighting and hunting
skills to equip them for adult life.

As a kitten grows

One day old

Newly born kittens cannot see and have very little control over their body movements.

Ten days old

A kitten's eyes usually open at about ten days.

Three weeks old

The kitten will start to experiment with solid food at this age.

Mother and baby care

Kittens are totally dependent on their mother and her milk for the first three weeks. After this, they begin to experiment with eating the solid food that their mother brings back in the form of prey for them to eat, or which their human carer provides. The mother will eat and drink more than normal to maintain a plentiful milk supply. Four good meals daily should be enough for her, depending on the number of kittens. The meals should be small and consist of fresh food, preferably one formulated for lactating queens, to make sure she receives the nutrients she needs to maintain her own body as well as her offspring.

Keeping kittens clean is a vital role for mothers, whose kittens may otherwise die of disease. The mother continues to wash them all over until the babies learn how to do this themselves.

Early learning

Begin to handle the kittens from two weeks old, to start the vital feline-human socialization process. At this age, the mother cat will not be too anxious about familiar humans touching her babies. By

Fourteen weeks old

The kitten's motor skills have improved, his ability to balance reaches a peak.

Five months old

Sexual maturity may be reached from this age, though it does vary from cat to cat.

Five weeks old

By now the kitten will be able to run and balance well.

Eight weeks old

The kitten will have learnt how to socialize with his siblings, and other pets in the household.

the age of three weeks, kittens can stand quite well and toddle around on short, unsteady legs. At this stage, they can roll over and right themselves, and play with their siblings, with paw pats and bites. By the fourth week, the kittens can move around confidently, and by the end of the fifth week they can often run and balance well. However, it will be another five to six weeks before they can run, jump and leap with accuracy, balance and co-ordination.

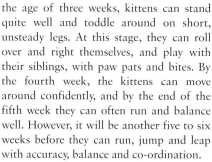

Adult cat

Full size and maturity are reached at about one year of age.

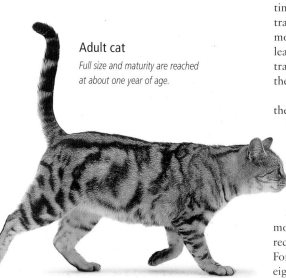

Weaning

At four weeks, the kittens start to explore outside the nest, and experiment more with solid food (see pages 20–21 for feeding guidance). Supply them with food specially formulated for kittens to make sure they receive the nutrients their rapidly growing bodies need.

As they eat increasing amounts of solids, their excreta changes and their mother stops cleaning up after them – so now it is time to provide them with their own litter tray. If they do not learn to use it from their mother, place them on it after every meal; leaving a small amount of excreta in the tray from their last elimination will help them recognize where to go at first.

Queens naturally wean their kittens themselves as their milk gradually dries up five to six weeks after the birth. At this age, the kittens should be fully weaned on to solid kitten food, although they may still return to mum for the occasional comfort suckle if she allows it. By eight weeks, the kittens are usually fully independent of their mother as regards food and hygiene requirements, and are ready for rehoming. For information about cat behaviour from eight weeks onwards, see pages 28–33.

FIRST AID AND ILLNESS

Despite your best attention, things can always go wrong, and it is wise to be ready for any eventuality concerning the health of your cat. Try to minimize the possibility of accidents occurring around your home, and be vigilant about keeping an eye out for any signs of ill health that may need addressing.

First aid

A knowledge of first aid can prove useful, and in some instances essential. Accidents tend to happen when we least expect them to, so it is sensible to be prepared. Emergency situations need immediate action; if you know what to do you may be able to limit the injuries sustained by your pet, and perhaps even save his life.

First-aid training

Having basic first-aid training will give you the confidence to deal with an emergency calmly and efficiently until an expert can take over. Some vet clinics run courses in basic first aid, and it is worth enlisting on one of these. Practising first-aid procedures on a healthy cat when you are not under pressure is a good way to learn what to do in a real situation.

First-aid kit

It is useful to have a home first-aid kit with which to treat minor injuries, to minimize adverse effects on the cat. Basic first-aid items can be bought from your vet, local pharmacy or good pet shops. A first-aid kit should contain the following:

It is important to keep a basic first aid kit close to hand so that you are prepared for an emergency situation.

- **absorbent kitchen paper** to wipe up any liquid mess.
- **antihistamine** to ease insect stings/bites.
- **antiseptic lotion** for cleaning wounds – particularly animal bites.
- **antiseptic wound powder** for treating wounds.
- **bandages** to keep dressings in place.
- **cat claw-clippers** (guillotine type).
- **conforming ('sticky') bandage** – useful for holding dressings in place.
- **cotton buds** – dampen these and use to remove grass seeds or other objects from the eyes, to clean wounds and apply ointments.
- **cotton wool** to bathe eyes, clean wounds and use as a dressing – always dampen cotton wool before use.
- **curved, round-ended scissors** to clip fur and trim dressings to size.
- **Elizabethan collar** to prevent a cat interfering with dressings or stitches.
- **glucose powder** – mix a tablespoon of glucose with a teaspoon of salt in 1 litre (1¼ pints) of warm water to make a rehydrating fluid for cats.
- **heavy-duty protective gloves** to use when restraining a cat.
- **lubricant jelly** to lubricate the thermometer before insertion.
- **nonstick dressings** – for cuts.
- **pencil torch and batteries** to inspect the mouth and ears.
- **round-ended tweezers** to remove insect stings.
- **small stainless steel or plastic bowls** for saline or antiseptic solutions when bathing wounds.
- **space blanket or sheet 'bubble wrap'** to maintain body temperature in cases of shock and hypothermia.
- **squares of clean cotton** (old linen or cotton sheets are ideal) to place over wounds or stem blood flow.
- **sterile eye wash** – contact-lens saline solution can be used.
- **sticky surgical tape** to hold wound dressings in place.
- **surgical gloves** for use when treating wounds.
- **surgical spirit** to remove ticks.
- **syringe plunger** to administer liquid medicine.
- **table salt** to make a saline solution (2 teaspoons of salt dissolved in 1 litre [1¼ pints] of warm water) for cleaning wounds.
- **thermometer, rectal** You may prefer an aural thermometer, which is more expensive but easier to use.
- **towel** to wrap the cat in when administering medication, and also to restrain it in event of accident.

First-aid basics – ABC

The basics of first aid for a cat are ABC – airway, breathing, circulation. The first priority is to make sure that the cat's airway is clear, so that he is able to breathe, and that he is breathing. Next, check that his heart is beating. You can then deal with any other symptoms as appropriate.

Airway and breathing

If the cat has collapsed and is unconscious, check he is breathing. If there is little or no breathing and the tongue is blue-black, open the mouth and remove anything that is blocking the airway. Gently lift the chin to extend the cat's neck to open the airway. If he still does not breathe, the first step you should take is to administer artificial respiration, as follows:

1 Hold the cat's mouth shut and cover his nose with your mouth.
2 Gently breathe up the cat's nose – 30 breaths per minute (take your mouth from his nose between breaths to allow him to exhale).
3 Keep this up until the cat begins to breathe, veterinary help arrives or you believe the cat to be beyond help.

A sick cat is seldom co-operative. He feels vulnerable and defensive, so beware of his claws and teeth when handling him or doing something he does not feel happy with. Always wrap him in a towel for your own protection.

Circulation

Having administered artificial respiration, check for a heartbeat. Do this by putting your ear on the cat's chest on the left-hand side, just behind his elbow, and you will be able to hear it. Check for a pulse – place a couple of fingers in the same place as you put your ear, or on the inside of the cat's thigh in the groin area. If there is no heartbeat, begin chest compression:

1 Place one hand on either side of the cat's chest, just behind his elbows.
2 Squeeze the chest in a smooth action, giving two compressions every second (use the flat of the hand – never the fingers). Do not use too much force, as it is easy to break the ribs.
3 Give two breaths to the cat for every four compressions. Keep this up until the cat's heart begins to beat or a vet takes over and you cannot do any more. Keep checking for a heartbeat or pulse throughout this heart massage process.

Moving an injured cat

Approach the injured cat carefully, and also assess any danger to both yourself and the cat. Speak softly and reassuringly to him to help soothe him and keep him calm.

If the cat is in the road, move him to the side, if it is safe. The best way move him is to slide a board under him as a makeshift stretcher, or slide both hands under him, keeping him in a horizontal position. A common injury in road accidents is a ruptured diaphragm, so it is important to keep the cat horizontal to stop his internal organs moving.

Emergency situations

Advice on what to do in a number of situations requiring first aid is given below.

Road accidents

Check for obvious signs of injury; inspect the back of the neck for lumps and swellings that may show broken bones or other trauma. Seek veterinary attention as soon as possible, informing the vet of any signs of injury you have spotted. Even if the cat appears to have no external injury, a thorough veterinary check-up is essential in case there is internal haemorrhaging, which could be life-threatening if not detected and treated as soon as possible.

Burns and scalds

Cool the burn with iced water (if you can stand the cat in a bath or sink, pour this on for about 10 minutes) to reduce the pain and the severity of the burn. Cover the burn lightly with a cool, damp, clean cloth (handkerchief or tea towel), wrap the cat in a space blanket, place him in a warm carrier and take him to the vet without delay.

Chemical burns

Put rubber gloves on and wash the area under cold running water – stand the cat in the bath or sink and run water over the burn, or use a hose in the garden. Stop the cat licking the area and follow the instructions for burns and scalds.

Sunburn

Treat as for burns and scalds.

Poisoning

If you suspect your cat has ingested a poison (profuse salivating is the most obvious sign; extreme sleepiness is another and is commonly associated with rat poison), contact your vet immediately, giving the name of any poison you suspect. This will allow the practice to obtain any relevant information from the manufacturer while you are taking your cat to the surgery. If you are instructed by the vet to make your cat vomit, in order to rid his digestive system of as much of the poison as possible, place one or two small washing soda (sodium carbonate) crystals, if you have them, at the back of the cat's throat.

Alternatively, use mustard or salt mixed with a little water. Get the cat to the veterinary surgery without delay.

Broken bones

Signs of fractured bones – apart from them protruding through the skin – include extreme pain on moving a limb, swelling, tenderness, loss of control of and deformity of the limb, unnatural movement of the limb, or the sound of the two ends of the bone grinding against each other. Keep the cat as quiet and warm as possible and take him to a vet immediately.

Electrocution

Once the power is switched off, check that the cat is breathing – if not, begin artificial respiration (see page 101). If it is not possible to switch off the power supply, do not approach the cat. Electrocution will almost inevitably cause burns, which will need treating as detailed above.

Insect stings and bites

A cat will frantically claw at the area where he has been stung. If the cat has been stung in the throat, seek immediate veterinary attention, as swelling may block the airway. For stings elsewhere on the body, clip the fur from around the affected area, and wash it with saline solution. Bees leave their sting in the victim, but wasps do not. If you can see the sting, and it is removable with tweezers, do so carefully, and wipe the area with cotton wool dampened with surgical spirit.

Neutralize the effect of a wasp sting with vinegar or lemon juice; use bicarbonate of soda dissolved in a little water for bee stings. Dry the area thoroughly, but gently, and apply a wet compress to reduce the irritation and swelling. For other insect bites, clean and dry the area, then apply antihistamine spray or ointment.

Animal bites

Cats are at risk from bites from other cats and rats. If you suspect your cat has been bitten by another cat, clip the fur away from around the bite and clean the wound thoroughly with saline solution, followed by dilute antiseptic lotion. Dry the area, then apply a liberal dusting of antiseptic wound powder. Repeat twice daily – it is important the wound is kept clean, or it may fester, become infected and result in an abscess.

Rat bites are especially dangerous, as these rodents carry diseases. Treat immediately as for cat bites, then take your pet to a vet who may administer an antibiotic injection and prescribe an antibiotic dusting powder for the wound.

Snake bites

You must keep the injured cat as calm as possible and prevent him running around, or even moving, as this will speed up the circulation of the venom around his body. Seek immediate veterinary attention.

Drowning

Pull the cat out of the water, and hold him upside down to drain the water from his lungs. Then lay him flat and rub his body fairly vigorously to promote respiration. If he is not breathing, start artificial respiration (see page 101) and get veterinary help as soon as possible.

Foreign bodies

In most cases, it is best to leave the removal of foreign bodies to a vet – contact your veterinary clinic for advice. If the cat is pawing at the affected area, gently restrain him to prevent further damage until your vet takes over and deals with the problem. You can sometimes flush grass seeds out of the eye using a syringe filled with saline solution, and extract thorns from paws

fairly easily. Check that the end has not broken off. If it has, seek veterinary treatment, or it may fester.

Choking

Choking warrants immediate action: taking the cat to a vet will waste time and may result in asphyxiation. Wrap the cat in thick material and open his mouth to see if there is anything stuck in his throat. If you have a helper, ask them to hold his mouth open while you remove the blockage.

If whatever is blocking the airway is wedged in place, do not try to pull it, or you may cause more damage by pushing it in farther. Instead, with the cat on the floor in front of you but facing away from you, sit down, take the cat's hind legs and lift them to your knees, and hold the legs between your knees. Place one hand on either side of the chest and squeeze using jerky movements, to try to make the cat 'cough'. Squeeze about four or five times and the cat should cough out the object. Let your cat rest, then take him for a veterinary check-up. If the object does not come out, take the cat to the vet immediately.

Lameness

Check for foreign objects lodged in a limb or paw, and for broken bones. Seek veterinary attention as soon as possible.

Fits and convulsions

Limit how far the cat can move – put him in a large, padded cardboard box. Seek veterinary attention urgently. Seizures are potentially life-threatening.

Shock

Shock following an accident, injury or terrifying experience causes an acute fall in blood pressure, and is life-threatening. Signs of shock include: cool skin, pale lips and gums, faint, rapid pulse and staring but

unseeing eyes. Keep the cat quiet, wrap him in a space blanket, and promote blood circulation by gently but firmly massaging his body, taking care not to aggravate any injuries in doing so. Seek veterinary attention as soon as possible.

Fighting is usually a last resort in a territorial dispute, as close proximity to another fully armed and hostile cat is very dangerous.

Bleeding wounds

Most cuts and lacerations heal on their own fairly quickly; treatment consists simply of keeping them clean with cotton wool dampened with saline solution. Initial bleeding, which may be profuse, helps clean the wound of debris, lessening the risk of infection. Seek veterinary attention immediately, however, if:

• the wound is spouting bright red (arterial) blood in jets.

• there is a constant flow of dark red (venous) blood that will not stop.

• the wound is deep or serious enough to require stitching.

• gunshot wounds are suspected.

• the skin has been punctured – these wounds appear tiny on the surface, but can be quite deep and are thus particularly prone to becoming infected. Never attempt to remove a foreign object from such a wound as this may aggravate the injury and allow large amounts of bleeding (while in place, the object can act as a plug, preventing blood loss).

• cuts affect toes or a limb, as tendon damage may have occurred.

In minor wounds, you can stem the blood flow by means of gentle direct

DON'T MAKE IT WORSE!

- **Wounds**
  DON'T apply direct pressure to a wound with an object impaled in it, or with bone protruding from it, or attempt to remove any objects from wounds, since this may aggravate massive blood loss; leave this to a vet.

- **Severe bleeding**
  DON'T apply a tourniquet, since it can cut off the blood flow completely, causing severe – often life-threatening – danger to the cat.

- **Chest compression**
  DON'T attempt chest compression if a chest injury is suspected.

- **Choking**
  DON'T attempt to remove an object wedged in the mouth or throat, other than by the coughing method described on page 104. If this fails, leave it to a vet.

- **Burns**
  DON'T apply too much cold water at once to the affected area, since too sudden a drop in temperature may cause more disastrous problems. See page 103.

- **Electrocution**
  DON'T touch the cat without first switching off the power supply to prevent you also from being electrocuted.

- **Chemical burns**
  DON'T attempt to treat the cat without first putting on gloves and protective clothing, to prevent the chemicals burning you.

- **Fits and convulsions**
  DON'T attempt to hold down a fitting cat.

- **Fractures**
  DON'T try to splint a broken bone – leave this to a vet.

- **Poisoning**
  DON'T make the cat vomit unless the vet gives specific instructions on how to do so.

- **Fights**
  DON'T try to break up a cat fight using your hands – use a long broom-handle or stick to separate the cats.

- **Eye injuries**
  DON'T apply a bandage or compress to an eye if you suspect there may be a foreign body in it.

- **Ingested string**
  DON'T try to pull foreign bodies from the mouth or anus if you meet with resistance in doing so – seek veterinary attention instead.

pressure using a damp, clean pad of cotton material, before cleaning them. Where arterial or venous bleeding is present, apply indirect pressure (not on the wound itself) to the appropriate artery or vein if you can feel it under the skin on the heart side of the wound; otherwise press a cotton pad over the wound to help stem the flow of blood. Elevating the injury, if possible, will enable gravity to help reduce the blood flow.

Internal injuries

These can be detected by abnormal swelling of the abdomen; bleeding from the mouth, nose, ears, eyes, sex organs or anus; bloodstained urine and faeces; shock; or signs of bruising on the skin. Seek veterinary attention immediately.

Common illnesses

Cats suffer from a variety of illnesses, many of which can be treated successfully. You must seek veterinary advice and treatment quickly, and faithfully follow instructions given regarding medication and care. It will help the vet treat your cat more effectively if you can provide as many details as possible about your pet. This is where knowing your cat well can be, quite literally in some cases, a lifesaver.

Feline influenza
(feline respiratory disease/cat flu)

Flu in cats is not uncommon and in homes with more than one cat, and particularly in catteries, can soon spread to other cats. Generally, the mortality rate in cats infected by cat flu is low.

Cats normally spend a lot of time self-grooming. If your cat fails to stick to his usual hygiene routine, it may be a sign that all is not well.

Symptoms
These may include loss of appetite, fever, sneezing, depression, inflamed or reddened eyes, yellow or thick green discharge from the nose, occasional coughing and ulcers on the tongue.

Causes
The two main causes are viral. One is Feline Calicivirus (FCV). The other is feline herpes virus (FHV) or Feline Viral Rhinotracheitis (FVR). It is transferred from the affected cat through aerosol droplets from sneezes. Unfortunately, some cats are carriers, and although they do not show any signs of the condition they can still pass it to another cat.

What to do
Isolate an affected cat as soon symptoms appear and contact the vet within 24 hours. The incubation period is two to ten days, but even after successful treatment many cats are still carriers. It is best if the affected cat is not allowed to come into contact with another cat. Vaccinations – injected under the skin or sprayed up the cat's nose – can provide some protection.

Treatment
The first part of treatment is to nurse the cat to get him eating and drinking again, and the second is to administer drugs. The vet may prescribe antibiotics and mucolytics (to help clear the mucus).

Halitosis (bad breath)
This is one of the most common mouth problems suffered by cats; most show symptoms before they are three years old.

Symptoms
Foul breath, tender gums, loss of appetite and excessive drooling, as well as plaque and calculus (a build-up of minerals) on a cat's teeth can lead to heart and kidney disease if untreated. Yellow-brown stains on the teeth where they meet the gums are a classic symptom.

Accustom your kitten to having his teeth cleaned from the start, so that he comes to view it as a normal process. (See Brushing teeth on page 67).

Causes

The causes of halitosis is usually gingivitis (inflammation of the gums), or food trapped between the teeth that attracts bacteria and causes tooth decay. It is also a symptom of renal failure.

What to do

Clean and inspect the cat's teeth regularly as a preventative measure. Take your cat for a regular check-up which includes a mouth examination.

Treatment

If your cat has gingivitis, an antiseptic spray in his mouth may help. Ask the vet for advice on this. Provide some crunchy food (kibble or biscuit-type feed) at every mealtime, as this will help clean teeth. Feline 'dental toys', if the cat will play with them, may also help.

Vomiting

This is a symptom of another condition and not an illness in itself.

Symptoms

A forceful expulsion of the contents of the cat's stomach and small intestine through the mouth.

Causes

These include: a sudden change in diet; motion sickness; heatstroke; conditions that affect the chemical composition of the blood, such as diabetes mellitus, renal failure, liver disease or a bacterial infection; a foreign body in the stomach; gastric dilation/torsion, stomach cancer; parasitic worms; fear and stress; trauma to the head; infections; ingestion of emetic substances, such as grass, and furballs.

What to do

If your cat suddenly and repeatedly vomits, withhold food and water, and contact the vet. Keep the cat in view, covering the floor with newspaper, or something similar. Note when he vomits, and the consistency, colour and quantity of the vomit. By doing this, you will help the vet to find the cause and therefore treat the problem effectively. Occasional vomiting is normal. In cases of recurring vomiting, where large amounts of vomit are produced, or there is blood in the vomit, seek veterinary advice.

Vomiting that you consider to be a result of your cat's scavenging, and which is therefore spasmodic and not severe, is best treated by starving the cat for 24 hours, but offer him small amounts of water regularly, to help prevent dehydration.

After a day, reintroduce food with small, light meals, such as scrambled eggs or boiled chicken, gradually building up to his former regime. If the vomiting continues, or starts again when food is reintroduced, seek veterinary advice as soon as possible.

You can help prevent some of the causes of vomiting by treating your cat on a regular basis for internal parasites (worms), discouraging him from scavenging, not making sudden changes to his diet, not feeding him before travelling, and not overfeeding him.

Treatment

In cases of severe vomiting, the cat may be placed on an intravenous drip to keep him hydrated. Where a foreign body is wedged somewhere in the digestive system, surgery will be needed to remove it.

Diarrhoea

Like vomiting, diarrhoea is a symptom of an underlying condition and is not an illness in itself.

Symptoms

Pungent, liquid-like faeces; passed frequently, necessitating many trips to the litter tray, or appear as 'accidents'. If your cat is suffering from colitis (an inflamed colon), his faeces will contain quite a lot of mucus and bright red blood. Another symptom of colitis is tenesmus, where the cat strains to defecate. Diarrhoea often leads to dehydration, so your cat may appear slightly disorientated.

Causes

Diarrhoea may be a symptom of overeating, stress, intestinal worms, foreign bodies in the digestive system or fungal infections.

What to do

Prevent the cat from eating anything, but ensure that he is given adequate drinking water. If the diarrhoea is acute, provide the cat with a rehydrating fluid (see First-aid kit

on pages 100–101) and contact the vet. Keep your cat where you can see him, covering the floor with newspapers. Note the times of his motions, and the consistency, colour and quantity of the diarrhoea. By doing this, you will help the vet to find the cause and treat the problem effectively.

Treatment

The treatment for diarrhoea depends upon the underlying cause. If it is due to internal parasites, then anthelmintics (wormers) will be used to rid the cat of the infestation, while antibiotics will be used for infections. Diarrhoea can cause the cat to dehydrate, and can lead to irreparable body damage (particularly of the kidneys). In cases of severe diarrhoea (where overeating is not the cause), if it persists, or if there is blood in the motions, consult your vet.

Enteritis

This is inflammation of the intestines, causing diarrhoea.

Symptoms

Diarrhoea, and signs of blood in the loose motions.

Causes

Enteritis is very common among young cats and can be caused by different things, but the bacterium *Escherichia coli* (or E. coli) is often the culprit. Another major cause of enteritis is campylobacter bacteria.

What to do

Observe your cat's actions, and the amount, colour, consistency and smell of his motions. Look for any signs of blood.

Treatment

A broad-spectrum antibiotic together with regular doses of kaolin may resolve the condition. Sometimes more than one antibiotic or more than one course is needed. Enteritis can be life-threatening, therefore it is important to start treatment as soon as possible.

Constipation

Constipation is a failure by the cat to pass faeces (or passing fewer motions, and less frequently than usual). It is a symptom, not a disease, which may have many underlying causes, and is fairly common in elderly cats.

Symptoms

A cat producing extremely dry faeces, or straining to defecate, is probably constipated. Every cat and his lifestyle is different, but cats should be expected to defecate one to four times daily.

Causes

Any debilitating disease can cause constipation, as can a foreign body blocking the cat's digestive system. Constipation can also be a symptom of prostate problems in male cats.

What to do

Providing your cat with a diet high in fibre and giving a good overall balanced diet will help prevent many cases of constipation.

Treatment

If there is internal blockage, the cat will need surgery. In cases linked with diet, laxatives and a change of food may be all that is needed. Constipation is potentially very dangerous, so always consult your vet.

Urinary incontinence

This is the inability to control urination.

Symptoms

The cat will have 'accidents', often when resting. He will not have urinated deliberately, but the urine will dribble out involuntarily when he is lying down.

Causes

Possible causes include faulty urethral valves, congenital defects of the cat's urinary system, urolithiasis (crystals or 'stones' of insoluble calcium in the urinary system), cancer or prostate problems (in male cats). Urinary incontinence is seen particularly in older queens.

What to do

When taking your cat for an examination, provide a fresh sample of your pet's urine; this will reveal if any diseases are causing the problem. Change bedding at regular intervals, preferably daily. Do not get angry with the cat; he cannot help it.

Treatment

Surgery may be needed to treat faulty urethral valves, congenital defects of the cat's urinary system, urolithiasis, cancer or prostate problems, while drug therapy may be used to improve the effectiveness of the urethra in sealing the flow of urine. Urinary incontinence is not life-threatening in itself, but it is better to seek veterinary advice sooner rather than later.

Arthritis

This is an inflammation of the joints. There are two forms of arthritis that may affect cats – osteoarthritis and traumatic arthritis.

Symptoms

Swollen joints, difficulty in walking and lameness.

Causes

Osteoarthritis may be a condition in itself or a result of other conditions. It is a progressive and painful disease that will seriously affect the cat's quality of life. It may affect one or more joints, and the seriousness of the condition will depend on which joints are affected, and the general health of the cat. Osteoarthritis is not nearly as common in cats as it is in dogs. Overweight cats are more prone to osteoarthritis. Traumatic arthritis is a direct result of an injury to the joint.

What to do

Don't wait until your cat cannot walk before consulting the vet. Your vet will advise you on what action you should take, as this will depend on the underlying causes and treatment being given.

Treatment

The treatment for arthritis may include anti-inflammatory drugs and painkillers or, in some cases, surgery. A physical examination and observation of the cat's movement, along with X-rays and analysis of joint fluid, will give the vet an indication of how serious an arthritic problem is.

Poor exercise tolerance

Sometimes a normally active cat will develop problems that make exercise difficult for him.

Symptoms

Pain and discomfort during what should be normal exercise.

Causes

This is often a direct result of inflammation of the joints (arthritis). Where a muscle is diseased (for example with a bacterial infection), it is referred to as myopathy; where a muscle is inflamed, it is referred to as myositis.

What to do

Be very careful in administering painkillers, and do so under veterinary instruction.

They can lull a cat into a false sense of security, causing him to use injured joints which will result in more damage.

Treatment

In cases of mild myopathy, for example where your cat develops a slight limp for 24–36 hours, simply resting him will probably relieve the problem (it may be necessary to confine him). If the limp persists beyond this time, veterinary advice and treatment should be sought. When a joint is damaged, the injury is referred to as a sprain, and may involve damage to cartilage and ligaments. While not dangerous in itself, the condition is painful. If not treated adequately, a sprain may lead to osteoarthritis. Damage from osteo-arthritis is usually permanent.

Blindness

This may mean limited vision, or total lack of vision.

Symptoms

Your cat may bump into furniture and objects for no apparent reason. An elderly cat may have more problems with his eyesight in bright light and in darkness.

Causes

There is a variety of causes – from injury to hereditary diseases and conditions. As cats age, it is quite common for a bluish colour to appear in the eyes as the lens deteriorates.

What to do

Any cat showing symptoms of failing eyesight should be taken to a vet without delay.

Treatment

This depends upon the cause, but many cases of total blindness are untreatable.

Feline chlamydial infection

Chlamydia consists of infection with *Chlamydia psittaci*, a bacterium that causes conjunctivitis.

Symptoms

Conjunctivitis (reddened eye) and a thick, ocular discharge. Sneezing and a nasal discharge are also common.

Causes

Cats become infected by *Chlamydia psittaci*, which is spread by other infected cats.

What to do

Seek urgent veterinary treatment.

Treatment

The vet can prescribe antibiotics, and the whole course must be completed. If feline chlamydial infection is not treated quickly and adequately by a vet, it can infect the gastrointestinal (digestive) and genital systems of the cat, and may cause reproductive problems in queens.

If your cat scratches himself constantly, check his coat for signs of ear mites and fleas.

Ear mites

These insect parasites are common in cats.

Symptoms

Persistent ear-scratching. A build-up of wax in the ears, dotted with black specks, is an indication that a cat may have ear mites. The mites can move down the ear canal and infect the middle ear; such an infection will cause the affected animal to lose his sense of balance. The cat may be unable to hold his head straight or may constantly fall over.

Causes

Ear mites (*Otodectes cynotis*), which are common in cats and also in wild rodents.

What to do

Seek veterinary advice in all cases of ear mites, or if your cat suffers a loss of balance. All animals that have been in contact with the infected cat must also be treated, as ear mites can infect other animals and symptoms may take some time to show.

Treatment

In mild cases, the vet can prescribe ear drops. If the ears are irritated, anti-inflammatory drugs may be prescribed. Mites are easily treated if detected early enough. The ear mites are usually white or colourless and are not visible to the naked eye. A special instrument called an otoscope is used to inspect the inside of a cat's ears.

Ear canker (otitis)

An inflammation of the skin lining the ear, otitis is one of the most common conditions in cats, and may occur in one or both ears.

Symptoms

These may include regular ear-scratching and head-shaking, a discharge or smell from the ear and reddening of the inner ear flap and ear hole. The cat may well hiss at anyone who touches him around the ear.

Causes

Excess wax causes irritation, and the ear is stimulated to produce even more wax. This leads to ideal conditions for normally harmless fungi and bacteria to grow and prosper. Ear mites, foreign bodies in the ear and skin problems can also cause otitis.

What to do

Take any cat showing any of the symptoms of irritated ears to the vet as soon as possible – immediately if you suspect a foreign body is lodged in the ear. *Never* attempt to remove a blockage yourself, as you may damage the cat's ear permanently. Don't put any liquid, ointment or other medication inside the cat's ears unless directed by your vet, and don't put any solid object inside the cat's ear, including cotton buds, which may also damage the ear.

The ear should not be interfered with until your vet has had a chance to see it, as this may provide clues about the problem.

Treatment

Treatment may include syringing or the application of a topical medicine, such as ear drops or ointment. Whatever medication is prescribed, it is important that you administer it exactly as instructed, and always finish the course of treatment. In cases of recurring otitis, surgery may be necessary to improve ear ventilation. Even though otitis is not a serious condition, if not properly treated it can become chronic, causing severe problems and possibly damage to the ear and the cat's hearing.

Ear flap wounds

These are scratches or tears to the ear flaps (pinnas).

Symptoms

Any ear wound, no matter how minor, is likely to bleed a great deal. Even if the actual wound does not cause the cat any real pain, the irritation of blood running down the ear is likely to cause him to scratch at his ear and shake his head.

Causes

Ear flaps are often bitten and scratched in fights, and some cats may injure their ear flaps in their day-to-day life.

What to do

Clean the wounds using saline solution. Once cleaned, it will be possible to see the extent of the damage; if this is significant, seek veterinary treatment as the wounds may need suturing. After cleaning with saline solution, cover minor wounds with antiseptic ointment, cream or powder.

Treatment

If the wounds look inflamed within a few days of the injury, consult the vet, as antibiotic treatment may be required.

Kidney (renal) failure

Kidney failure is probably the most common problem in elderly cats. It is also a symptom of Polycystic Kidney Disease (PKD), a hereditary condition often found in Persian cats.

Symptoms

These include a seemingly insatiable thirst, the passing of large amounts of urine either in one go or at very frequent intervals, vomiting, diarrhoea, loss of appetite, weight loss, halitosis and anaemia.

Causes

For various reasons, the nephrons (parts of the kidneys that remove waste products from the blood) may fail to do their job properly, and this leads to chronic renal failure. This is an extremely serious, usually irreversible condition with a very poor chance of recovery. It rarely occurs in cats under 5 years of age.

What to do

Renal failure is life-threatening. Don't hesitate to contact the vet if you suspect this condition in your cat.

Treatment

Treatment of an affected cat may include a period of intensive care, during which the cat will have fluids administered via an intravenous drip, and a special diet, coupled with a restful lifestyle and medication. A cat with complete renal failure will die, and you may choose to have him put to sleep.

Feline infectious enteritis (FIE)

Also called feline panleukopenia, this life-threatening viral disease attacks the white blood cells and the cat's gut.

Symptoms

These include loss of appetite, persistent vomiting and diarrhoea.

Causes

The virus is passed from one infected cat to others.

What to do

This disease is highly infectious, so isolate an infected cat. Make sure all your cats are vaccinated and receive regular boosters.

Treatment

There is no real treatment for FIE, but special care and intensive nursing may alleviate the symptoms. Seek immediate veterinary treatment for any cat showing symptoms of this disease. A severe infection may kill a young cat or kitten very quickly.

Diabetes mellitus (sugar diabetes)

The cat is unable to control his blood-sugar levels.

Symptoms

Increased appetite, particularly if coupled with other symptoms such as an increase in the amount of urine passed, lethargy and weight loss. Symptoms of diabetes mellitus are often seen in queens just after they have started oestrus.

Causes

A lack of insulin (produced by the pancreas) or an increase in blood-sugar levels (hyperglycaemia). It is most common in cats over 8 years of age. Due to the increased levels of the hormone progesterone in the blood during phantom pregnancies, unspayed queens are said to be more than three times more susceptible to diabetes mellitus, and obese cats of either sex are also at increased risk.

What to do

Take any cat showing symptoms of diabetes to the vet as soon as possible.

Treatment

Treatment for this condition is likely to be long-term, as your cat may need regular insulin injections and other treatment, so the costs will be fairly high. Typically, you will need to collect and test a sample of urine from your cat every morning to check the glucose levels, calculate the amount of insulin needed and administer it by injection, and feed your cat an extremely regulated (high-fibre) diet at specific times. In queens, spaying will help to keep the cat's condition stable.

Diabetes insipidus

This renders the body incapable of regulating the use of water.

Symptoms

These include polydipsia (excessive thirst) and polyuria (production of large amounts of urine).

Causes

Diabetes insipidus is caused by lack of the Anti-Diuretic Hormone (ADH) or the failure of kidneys to respond to this hormone. Normally, the production of ADH is increased when there is little water intake, and decreased when the cat drinks large quantities of water, thus controlling the body's water balance.

What to do

Any sign of abnormal water intake should be investigated by a vet as soon as possible.

Treatment

Depending on which form of diabetes inspidus is present, treatment may involve the administration of ADH to the cat through nasal drops.

Abnormal water intake

This is an increased or decreased need to drink water.

Symptoms

The cat drinks either more or less water than usual. Other symptoms include increased or decreased urination.

Causes

It can be a symptom of cystitis, tapeworm infestation, diabetes insipidus or diabetes mellitus.

What to do

Keep an eye on urine deposits in the litter tray; if you know what is normal for your pet, a change will be detected early. Cystitis is indicated by discomfort and straining to urinate, while tapeworm is signalled by the visible presence of worms in faeces, and also tiny white segments of them sticking to fur around the anus.

Treatment

Take your cat for an examination: treatment will depend on the cause of the condition. If tapeworms are to blame, deworming will be in order, while cystitis is treatable with antibiotics.

Feline leukaemia virus (FeLV)

This viral infection affects the cat's immuno-response system.

Symptoms

Lethargy, high temperature, lack of appetite and enlarged lymph nodes in the neck, 'armpits' and groin area.

Causes

A virus which is contained in blood, semen and saliva; it is spread through mating and bite wounds.

What to do

There can be a delay of as much as three years between the cat becoming infected and showing signs of the condition, so there is no real urgency to seek veterinary treatment unless the cat exhibits severe symptoms that cause him pain or discomfort.

Treatment

There is no cure for FeLV. Many cats infected with the disease will make a reasonable recovery naturally, but will become carriers, spreading the condition to other cats. If you have more than one cat, the vet may recommend that the infected cat is put to sleep to prevent the infection spreading. If you have just one cat, you must not allow him to go outside. Some owners prefer not to risk their cat infecting others, so choose to have him put to sleep. A vaccine is available, and owners are advised to have their cat vaccinated on a regular basis.

Feline infectious peritonitis FIP)

Caused by a virus that affects cats under about three years of age, this infection spreads rapidly among cats, and so is particularly dangerous in multi-cat homes.

Symptoms

Loss of appetite and weight, swollen abdomen, breathing problems and fever.

Causes

A virus (feline coronavirus) passed from an infected cat.

What to do

Isolate infected cats and seek urgent veterinary advice.

Treatment

There is no treatment for FIP and most cats die as a direct result of this infection. It may be advisable to have your cat put to sleep; your vet will help you to make this decision.

Feline immunodeficiency virus (FIV)

Also known as feline T-lymphotropic lentivirus (FTLV) and feline AIDS, this viral infection affects the RNA (ribonucleic acid) involved in the manufacture of proteins in the cat's cells. It prevents the body's immuno-defence system fighting infections.

Symptoms

This virus allows many infections to become established in the affected cat but has no symptoms as such.

Causes

The virus multiplies in the white cells in the cat's blood and is often transmitted through cat bites.

What to do

You must take any cat suspected of suffering from FIV to the local vet. Infected cats will suffer chronic long-term illness, weight loss and other debilitating conditions as a result of the infections caused by lack of immuno-response.

Treatment

There is currently no treatment available for a cat infected with FIV and euthanasia is usually recommended.

Obesity

Many owners overfeed and under-exercise their pets, sometimes with the best of intentions and not realising the long-term impact on their health.

Symptoms

The cat is overweight, even grossly fat, with rolls of fat under the skin. This can cause breathlessness and reluctance to exercise. It can predispose the cat to joint problems and other illnesses associated with obesity, such as heart and major organ failure.

Causes

Old age, when the cat does not exercise as much as he once did; under-exercise in younger cats; overeating or being fed an unsuitable diet.

What to do

Consult your vet regarding a suitable diet plan that will ensure your cat gets the correct balance of nutrients from his food.

Treatment

Encourage your cat to exercise more by playing, and hide his food ration around the house so he has to hunt for it. Follow your vet's diet plan strictly; if your cat is old, a specially formulated, low-calorie diet will probably be recommended.

Heatstroke

A fever caused by failure of the body's temperature-regulating mechanism when exposed to excessively high temperatures.

Symptoms

Agitation and extreme distress. First, the cat will stretch out and pant heavily, then drool and stagger as if drunk. Finally, if untreated, it can collapse, pass into a coma and die.

Causes

Usually being in a car – either on a long journey or left inside one. Inside a car, there is poor ventilation and the temperature rises to a dangerous level quickly, even in the cooler sunshine of spring or autumn.

What to do

You must act fast. In mildly affected cats, move them to a cool place and ensure a steady passage of cool air.

Treatment

In bad cases, cool the cat down with cold water from a hosepipe (using a fine spray) or by gently pouring bowlfuls of cold water over him. In very bad cases, cover the cat with wet towels, including the head (keeping the nose and mouth clear) and keep dousing him with cold water. Seek veterinary assistance urgently. In all cases of heatstroke, it is vital to keep the head cool, as the brain may literally be cooked. Take particular care with white cats, especially the tips of the ear flaps.

Flea dermatitis

Irritation and soreness of the skin occurs around flea bites.

Symptoms

Red, raw areas and scabs caused by the cat scratching himself; these may be found all over the cat's body, or just in localized areas such as near the base of the tail and behind the ears. Some cats are more sensitive than others to flea bites and can be driven to distraction with the itching.

Causes

A reaction to the saliva of the fleas when they bite the cat.

What to do

Consult your vet.

Treatment

The cat may require treatment to alleviate irritation, kill the fleas and prevent reinfestation.

Ringworm

This is a fungal infection of the skin.

Symptoms

Scratching, and circular areas of hair loss, with the visible skin scaly and raised around the edge of the lesion.

Causes

Fungi, including *Microsporum canis*, *Microsporum gypseum* and *Trichophyton mentagrophytes*. Spores of these fungi may be wind-borne or found in the soil.

What to do

Some of the fungi responsible for ringworm can be contracted by humans, so take care that you and your family are not infected. Only your vet can prescribe effective treatment, so seek urgent advice.

Treatment

Wash the cat in fungicidal wash prescribed by a vet, who may also recommend topical applications of fungicidal ointment.

THE OLDER CAT

The company of an ageing cat in good health is delightful and soothing, and just as rewarding as playing with a kitten. To care for an older cat, you may need to make some changes in his everyday regime, and make a few allowances for his age, but it will be well worth the effort.

Caring for the older (senior) cat

A cat can be considered old when he starts to take things easy and spends more time than usual sleeping. The old cat's reactions are sharp, his movements are subtle, and he may even deign to chase string and pat feathers, as long as he is not made to feel foolish. Just because he sits around a lot and is undemanding and quiet, an elderly cat should not be ignored.

Lifestyle

Just like elderly people, old cats are resistant to and can be upset by major changes in their routine and lifestyle. If changes do have to happen, try to incorporate them gradually to allow your cat time to get used to them. Everything should be done to keep the elderly cat feeling as good as possible. (For holiday care, see pages 68–71.)

If your cat has disturbed behaviour patterns it may be the result of chronic illness. For example, a previously clean cat may have 'accidents', making puddles on chairs and carpets. Should this happen, it may be best to keep the cat in areas of the house where such accidents don't matter – but that does not mean he should be shut away or limited in his access to his family, as this would be unfair and cruel. It would also be unfair and cruel to chastise or ban the cat from the house for something that is beyond his control. Carpets can be replaced, but loving companions cannot.

Companionship

Some people consider getting a kitten when their established cat gets old. This can be a good or bad decision, depending on the temperament and nature of the aged cat. If he likes

For an elderly person a more mature cat that is already house-trained and is more independent, may be easier to accommodate than a kitten.

the kitten, then he may gain a new lease of life. If, however, he does not, then he may resent the newcomer and become depressed and withdrawn, stop eating and, ultimately, become very ill. If the old cat is the only one in the household and has always been a loner, then it would be kinder not to get another cat or kitten.

If your elderly cat displays an increased need for your company, always give him plenty of attention and reassurance – even consider moving his bed into your bedroom at night, if necessary. Leaving a radio on with the volume turned down low while you are out can help provide 'company'.

Diet

Foods specially formulated for elderly cats are available, and these contain all the nutrients the ageing body needs to remain in the best possible condition, and help delay or alleviate the onset of conditions such as senility. As older cats can often

Older cats seek out warm places to rest – on top of a boiler being a favourite spot – because their bodies do not regulate temperature as efficiently as their younger counterparts.

suffer from urinary-tract problems, a totally dry diet may not be the best choice; it may be wise to consult your vet regarding the best type of food for your cat. See also Feeding your cat, pages 20–21.

Bad teeth and inflamed gums are not uncommon in old cats; at this stage, your cat will find soft moist or semi-moist food easier to eat. Make sure there is always a plentiful supply of fresh, clean water.

An older cat may not be able to defend his food as well as he once could, so if you have other cats and dogs ensure they are not allowed to steal his meals, or intimidate him while he is eating and scare him off.

Being less active as he grows older, it is easy for the cat to pile on weight, which can put undue strain on his heart and joints; keep a careful watch on this. Equally, he

could lose weight rapidly and starve if he is not eating for some reason. Weighing your cat once a week can help you monitor his weight – and this is quite simple to do. First, weigh yourself on your bathroom scales, and then weigh yourself again while holding the cat; deduct the first weight from the second to ascertain your pet's weight. It may be easier for a helper to read the weights while you stand still on the scales.

Keep an eye on senior cats when they are allowed outside, particularly senile, blind or deaf pets – these are at risk of getting lost and potential hazards such as predators.

Food specially formulated for elderly cats is available. These foods contain all the necessary nutrients to help them remain in the best possible condition.

Older cats are prone to constipation. Seek veterinary attention if this occurs.

Common ailments

As a cat ages, his body tissue starts to degenerate. This is inevitable and cannot be prevented, although with care from both owner and vet the effects can be eased. Elderly cats are prone to a number of particular ailments:

• claw damage, owing to a decreasing ability to retract the claws efficiently.
• coat and skin complaints, owing to inefficient self-grooming.
• cold-related problems, owing to decreased body temperature regulation.
• constipation, owing to decreased digestive efficiency.
• deafness.
• heart disease.
• high blood pressure (hypertension).
• incontinence.
• increased predisposition to furballs.
• injury, owing to decrease in agility.
• joint stiffness and arthritis.
• kidney disease.
• liver failure.
• loss of appetite.
• obesity-related problems.
• senility.
• sight problems.
• tooth and gum problems.

Seek veterinary advice for all of these ailments – the more quickly they are dealt with the more likely it is that the treatment will be successful, and your cat's comfortable life prolonged.

Time to say goodbye

Eventually the older cat sleeps more and more, and is increasingly reluctant to exercise. He may drink lots of fluids, but may take little solid food. While he is able to function normally, if only in this modified way, he is probably quite contented. If his bladder and bowels begin to fail and he is unable to eat, you must seek veterinary advice, for the only humane thing to do in these circumstances is to have your old cat put to sleep, allowing him to die painlessly and with dignity. It is the last, kind thing you can do for a much-loved companion and friend. Refer to pages 124–125 for information on bereavement and euthanasia.

Bereavement

When a companion animal dies, or his death is imminent, this often has a huge impact on those humans who loved and cared for him. Losing a much-loved pet is for many owners comparable with coping with the death of a family member or close friend. Individual people deal with this trauma in different ways.

Why pet cats die

There are two main reasons for a cat dying:
• sudden death through accident or illness.
• euthanasia (being 'put to sleep' or 'put down') following an accident, or because of old age or illness, which prove to not be treatable and the cat's quality of life is or will be poor.

The former will no doubt come as a huge shock, while in the latter, you can prepare for the inevitable, although it is no easier to bear. The important thing is to focus on the many happy times you enjoyed with your pet.

Euthanasia

Other than sudden death, bringing your cat's life to a peaceful end is the most humane way for him to die. A prolonged natural death can be traumatic for both of you, and painful for the cat.

Discuss with your vet whether having your cat put down at home or at the clinic would be more practical and what you want done with your pet's body. Once this has been mutually agreed, arrange a time, preferably sooner rather than later.

At the veterinary clinic

Arrange a time when the vet clinic is likely to be quiet, or you can enter and leave through a private entrance. Have a supportive person to take you there and back; you may be in no fit state to cope with

this by yourself. Take a blanket in which to wrap your pet to bring him home again, if this is what you want to do. Make the journey there as smooth, stress-free and quiet as possible. If you will be able to bear up in your pet's last moments, then be with him. If you feel you will go to pieces, then ask your vet and the vet nurse to deal with it; if you are distressed, it may make your pet equally so, and his passing may not be as peaceful as it should be.

At home

Ask for a veterinary nurse to accompany the vet to help out as required or where necessary, and help to keep you and the cat calm, thereby making the process as stress-free as possible. On the day, keep your cat's routine beforehand as normal, but give him lots of extra attention and cuddles if he will allow you to.

The process

The process is quick and relatively painless. The vet may administer a sedative if the cat is very distressed, difficult to handle or restrain. They usually shave a foreleg to locate the vein. They then inject a concentrated barbiturate (an anaesthetic overdose) into that vein. The cat almost immediately goes to sleep. Breathing swiftly ceases, and the heart stops beating.

If the circulatory system is not working efficiently, and therefore the necessary vein on the foreleg is not easy to find, the vet may need to inject directly into chest or abdomen. Owners may not be able to hold their pet and keep him calm, so this is where the experience of a veterinary nurse can help.

Afterwards

If you wish, the vet will arrange to have the body buried or cremated. Alternatively, you can take your cat home, if this is permitted, and bury him in the garden. Graves should be at least 1 m (3 ft 3 in) deep and well away from water courses (your local environment agency should be able to advise you where these are). If you decide to have the body buried or cremated, pet cemeteries and crematoriums will advise you on the costs, and what is involved.

Grief

Only the owner can understand how they feel after losing a pet that meant the whole world to them, and it is important to realize that grieving is an essential part of the healing process after bereavement. There is no set time limit as to how long owners should grieve.

Help when you need it most

Do not be afraid to lean on supportive family and friends when you feel the need, and do make use of the pet-bereavement support services that are available through phone, letter and email – many animal charities and some pet-insurance companies provide such a service, or go to see an understanding doctor or bereavement counsellor.

Marking your cat's passing with a grave and monument of some kind, whether a headstone, tree, shrub or plant, can prove therapeutic. You have somewhere tangible to go to mourn your pet, and then something to remember him by.

Children and pet loss

For many children losing a pet will be the first time they experience this inevitable part of life. It will help a parent to talk through what to say beforehand with a bereavement counsellor. The child may also find such supportive third-party help invaluable. One thing you should *not* do is say that the pet was 'put to sleep', as this can create false hope that their pet will wake up and come back.

Pet grief

It is not just the owner who grieves over the loss of a pet; so can other animals in the household. The best thing to do is to carry on with the remaining pets' routine as normal, and to let them work out a new hierarchy among themselves.

Time for a successor

Only you will know when the time is right to get another cat. When it is, remember that there are plenty of homeless felines, young and old, waiting in rescue centres to fill the gap in the life of a special someone who can offer them the life they deserve – a good, caring home and lots of love.

Index

Acknowledgements

Managing Editor Clare Churly
Editor Camilla Davis
Executive Art Editor Leigh Jones
Designer Jo Tapper
Picture Library Assistant
    Taura Riley
Assistant Production Controller
    Nosheen Shan

Picture credits
Octopus Publishing Group Ltd 9, 21, 28 bottom, 66; /Jane Burton 1, 2–3, 6, 8, 11,
17, 18, 19, 20, 26, 28 centre right, 29 bottom, 38 top, 48, 49, 50 top left, 50 bottom
right, 54, 55, 56, 58 top left, 58 top right, 58 bottom right, 58 bottom left, 61 top
left, 61 top right, 61 bottom right, 61 bottom left, 62, 64 top left, 64 top right, 64
bottom right, 64 bottom left, 65 bottom, 67, 73, 86 top right, 86 bottom left, 87
left, 87 right, 88, 90, 92, 93, 95 top, 96-97, 100, 108; /Steve Gorton 7, 10, 22, 23, 25,
27, 28 centre left, 30, 32, 33, 35, 36 top right, 36 bottom, 37 left, 39, 40, 41, 42, 43,
44, 45, 46, 51 top, 51 bottom, 53, 63, 69, 72, 83, 98, 105, 118, 120, 121, 122 top,
123, 125; /Peter Loughran 15 top, 99; /Ray Moller 12, 13, 14, 15 bottom, 28 top
right, 29 centre left, 29 centre right; /Dick Polak 102; /George Taylor 70; /Nick
Goodall 68; /Rosie Hyde/Stonehenge Veterinary Surgery 85.
Warren Photographic/Jane Burton 29 top.